- *Getting There* -
Visiting Fire Lookouts in Yakima County

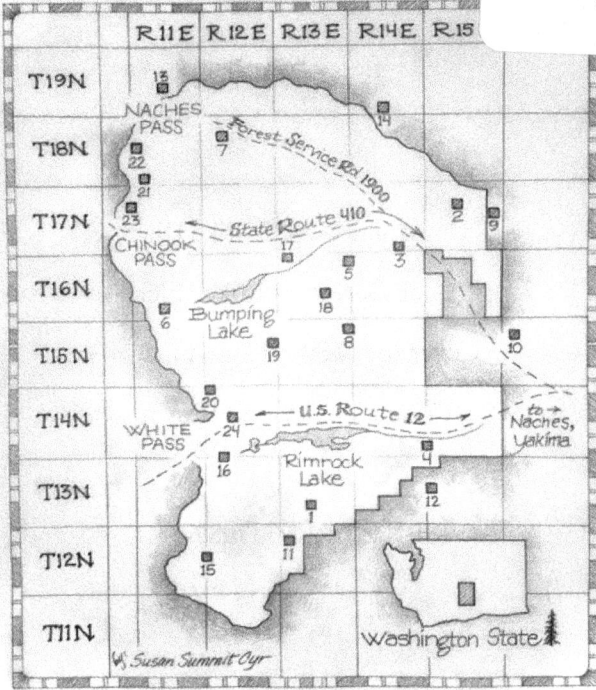

Mike Hiler

And friends

洞月亮

YAKIMA WASHINGTON

cavemoonpress.com 中 cavemoonpress@gmail.com

ISBN: 978-1-7337987-5-4

GETTING THERE

Visiting Fire Lookouts in Yakima County

Mike Hiler

2023

With Contributors Windy Warren, Mildred McMurray, and Earl Brown

Map by Susan Summit Cyr

洞月亮

YAKIMA WASHINGTON

cavemoonpress.com 中 cavemoonpress@gmail.com

Acknowledgements:

I would like to thank the many friends who helped this project including publisher Doug Johnson and my wife Kristin Hiler. Wendy Warren kindly contributed an article about her time on Pine Mt. Lookout. Her contribution makes this effort more timely, and inclusive as many women, over the years, have served as lookouts. Earl Brown's pen and ink drawings are remarkable and preserve important details of the local lookouts. I want to personally thank him and his wife Carolyn for permission to include those drawings in this book. The original drawings belong to the U. S. Forest Service and are displayed at the Naches Ranger Station.

The complete Mildred McMurray lookout diary is in the possession of the Naches Ranger Station and can be viewed there in their history files. Mildred passed away in 1992.

I want to thank the "editing readers" Bette Cooney and Barry Donahue for their tireless work in improving my rough document. I hope to have included most of their suggested improvements and any remaining typos are on me. I would also like to thank Bette for being instrumental in matting, framing, and presenting Earl's drawings at the Naches Ranger Station when she was the information specialist. Barry's hard work in field proofing portions of this text was invaluable.

I want to thank Susan Summit Cyr, author of "Tanum, A Story of Bumping Lake and the William O. Douglas Wilderness" for her encouragement and for her Beautiful "Getting There" cover map.

- Cover Art and maps by Susan Summit Cyr
- Lookout sketches by Earl Brown
- Lookout stories by Wendy Warren and Mildred McMurray
- Reading editors: Bette Cooney and Barry Donahue

Table of Contents

Lookout Stories:

ALPHABETICAL LISTING
OF LOOKOUTS

Historic Fire Lookout Stations and Observation Sites
Yakima County, Washington State

Naches Ranger District, U.S. Forest Service
and
Adjacent Yakima County Boundary Locations

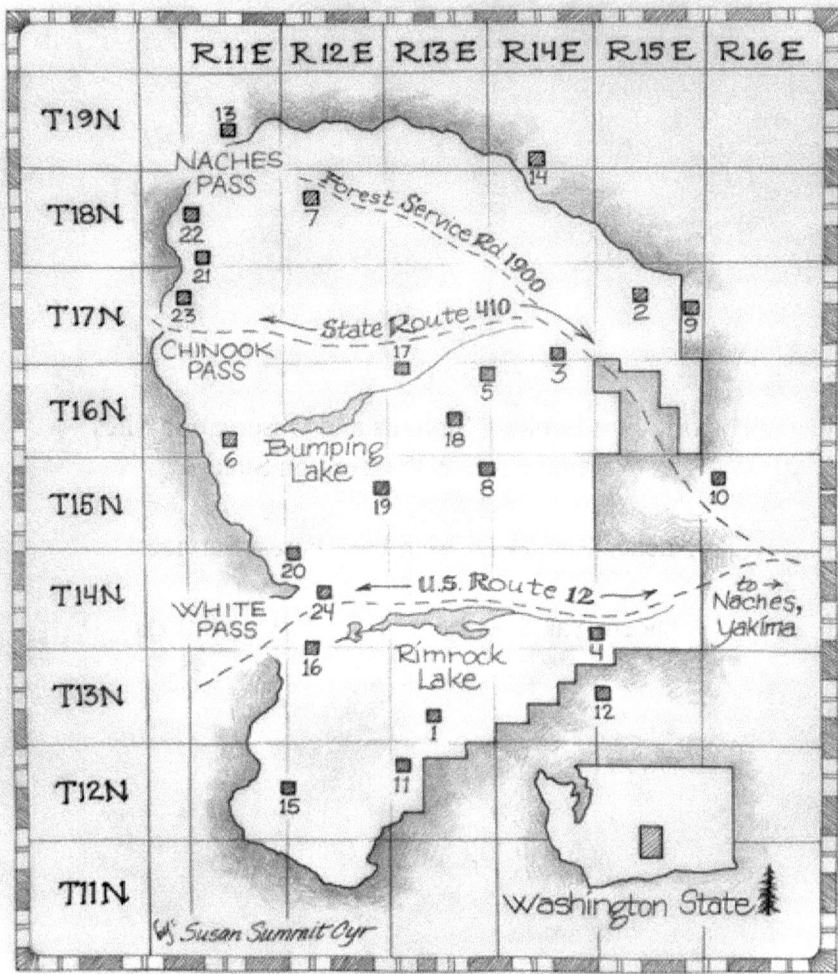

	R11 E	R12 E	R13 E	R14 E	R15 E	R16 E
T19N	13			14		
T18N	22	7				
T17N	21 23		17	3	2	9
T16N	6		5 18			
T15N			8		10	
T14N	20 24					
T13N	16		1	4 12		
T12N	15	11				
T11N						

NACHES PASS

Forest Service Rd 1900

State Route 410

CHINOOK PASS

Bumping Lake

WHITE PASS

U.S. Route 12

to → Naches, Yakima

Rimrock Lake

Washington State

W. Susan Summit Oyr

Introduction

The remote fire lookout station detection system is integral to the history of the U.S. Forest Service and other agencies managing public timberlands. The Naches Ranger District, located mostly in Yakima County and along the east side of the central Washington Cascades has hosted a number of lookout stations throughout the period between 1920 and 1990. Today, Jumpoff Lookout is the last remaining lookout station in Yakima County, though unstaffed. All the other Yakima sites are now abandoned.

Most of the old (but now gone) lookout station sites still retain evidence of their former use. Concrete foundations, discarded phone lines, debris, guy-wire cables, toilets, abandoned buildings, and the evidence of station removal (glass, nails, and other burned remains) are visible at most of the old abandoned sites. Two books have been written about Pacific Northwest Lookouts, and this information has fueled public interest in the old stations. While working on this project I have relied on these two books extensively and my appreciation goes out to Ira Spring for *Lookouts, Firewatchers of the Cascades and Olympics* (The Mountaineers, Seattle, WA 1981) and to Ray Kresek for his *Fire Lookouts in the Northwest* (Ye Galleon Press, Fairfield, WA, 1984) for salvaging lookout information that would otherwise be lost.

Lookout station sites across and adjacent to the Naches Ranger District offer a variety of visitor experiences as well as great views. Early stations were constructed at remote mountain peaks such as Mount Aix, Tumac Mountain, and Bear Creek Mountain, and those remote sites have since been included within Legislated Wilderness (1964 and 1984) to be protected in their natural condition. As the lookout system expanded in the 1930's, stations were placed at the ends of existing roads, or roads were pushed into the sites to make

1

them more serviceable. As a result, the sites today offer a wide spectrum of access type and opportunity for visitors, ranging from remote trailed sites, easier access trailed sites from paved roads, four-wheel driveway, 4x4 jeep trails, system forest gravel roads, and even a few cross country bushwhacking routes.

The Naches area lookout stations were located in a variety of land management allocations and adjacent and diverse ownership patterns. Some sites are on state or private land, some are on the Forest Service boundary and were administered by the Naches Ranger District or with adjacent Forest Service Districts. While some sites today have almost returned to their natural condition or reveal little trace of former use, others retain lasting evidence of the "Lookout Period".

While the Naches Ranger District lookout stations were once integral to a comprehensive agency fire detection system, their use has been displaced by the dictates of progress. This earlier program depended on the isolated lookout station and the lonesome "lookout" living there to relay information over single strand (bare) #9 wire telephones and (later on) crude radios. Their task was to detect and suppress wildfire, greet visitors and generally keep an eye on the large swaths of forest they were paid to oversee. I remember in the early seventies being requested by the Tieton District Range Administrator to keep an eye on permitted cattle, check brands, monitor unpermitted cattle, walk fences, inspect cattle guards, and help cowboys locate wandering open range livestock. Lookouts have been known to report the large dust cloud following sheep bands or dust rising from late summer dusty roads.

I also worked with game agents relaying information on possible poaching and animal movements. I maintained a spring exclusion fence, acted as a 24-hour a day radio monitor for backcountry patrols, and recorded weather and lightening for the fire suppression efforts. I kept an active visitor log and was expected to explain Forest policies to visitors and to help distressed or curious visitors at my remote location, along with washing windows. One of the former Miners Ridge lookouts remembered building a trail to Root Lake, a task consuming his evenings for an entire summer. Many lookouts had to carry their own water, split wood, and perform station maintenance.

Air patrol, improved radio communication, changing agency missions, increased public presence, better roads, changing public perception regarding vandalism, and increased personnel and payroll auditing were all a part of the progress which eventually squeezed the lookout station out of existence. Just as the pack string and the single strand telephone "land line" vanished, so did the lonely lookout station. But trend is not destiny; lookouts may one day see a revival. Today the old lookouts are an integral part of the Forest Service history and lore and the remaining sites are our primary link to a time when the Forest Service charge was much simpler than it is today. Some of the old stations themselves remain as an effective "interpretive" opportunity and visitors are now flocking to the old sties to stretch their legs, commune with what little is left, and enjoy the view. We also hope Appendix "C" will help visitors get home safely.

This collection of fire lookout stations on the Naches District has been compiled to stimulate interest in the old Yakima County sites, enhance cultural resource protection, and encourage public interpretive programs associated with these old places. The individual histories in this collection are rather condensed but hopefully more exhaustive research on individual stations will follow. The appendices in this text are included to establish a background of information for finding and visiting these sites and to encourage folks who want to *get there*.

The Osborne Firefinder: William B. Osborne, early forest Service Employee, invented and perfected the original and iconic "Osborne Firefinder" a unique, inspired and game changing device used by fire lookouts to transfer a fire's location to head quarters on a single strand phone line, and later, over the radio. It measures distance to the fire, elevation, and vertical and horizontal azimuth with remarkable accuracy and inspiring mechanical simplicity. A young firefighter can learn to use this device with a minimum of training, Cleaning, care, and maintenance is easy, and night-time service during a lightening storm is possible, though challenging, with just a candle. See Earl Brown's drawing of the inside of a lookout station and you will clearly see that the Osborne Firefinder is central, anchored in the center of the station where lookout life revolved around it. A picture of an Osborne Firefinder is incomplete without the obligatory cup of coffee.

ABOUT *"GETTING THERE"*

L ookout station sites across the Naches Ranger District offer a variety of visitor experiences. Some require a dedicated hike from a remote trailhead, but others can be reached with a family sedan. Some visits simply require a high road clearance car or truck, but others can only be visited with a short wheelbase, dedicated four-wheel drive jeep type vehicle. Jumpoff Lookout is an example of a lookout requiring jeep style 4x4 or motorbike access, but you can also visit it over forest system trails or cross country hike into the old station with a GPS. The road I found poorly maintained yesterday may just be ready for family sedans on the day of your visit.

The Naches District distributes two free *Recreation Guide* handouts for visitors who wish to find the old lookout sites. Titled *Road Trips on the Naches District* and *View Points and Fire Lookouts*, these guides direct Forest visitors to the sites or to trail-heads which access these old historic sites. The District Office, located in Naches, also sells a variety of plant and animal identification books to make lookout trips safer and more enjoyable. The *Naches District 1 inch to the mile Fireman's Map*, sometimes called the *District Recreation Map*, is invaluable in finding your way into these sites and getting back home. That one map is all anyone needs to visit the 24 lookouts ilustrated in this book.

Anomalies of lookouts include the various conflicting elevations printed in different books and web sites, the differences in the way county boundaries are interpreted, and the extent of photo panorama collections at individual Ranger Stations. Please refer to elevations and "year of occupancy" from primary source material when you can, and never stake your life on my numbers matching those of your favorite guide or GPS. Lookout stations weren't built in one day. In some cases the construction or removal of an individual lookout required several years of work which was seasonal in nature. Appendix B: *Lookout and Peak Elevations* is included to help and not hinder your visits but perhaps a good argument, among friends is part of what we take back home after a day of exploring.

NOTE: Please check my facts. As you read this book you may come upon questions or helpful corrections. Suggestions for further reading include the lookout books by Kresek and Ira Springs mentioned above. For more specific historic references of the Naches Area the Gretta Gossett book, *Beyond the Bend* contains volumes of scattered information to help you form a mental picture of the lookout era plus specific information on certain lookouts. And for "All out" reading enjoyment check out *Of Men and Mountains*, the first-hand, childhood memories of the Naches Basin by Supreme Court Justice William O. Douglas. It stands as a lonely peak, viewed from the distant past, written by someone who was there.

USING THIS GUIDE

This guide offers some historical information along with travel guide directions to simplify a visit to the Forest Service managed (or shared) Yakima County Historic Fire Lookout Sites. Because nearby viewpoints also offer outstanding views and, because they were also used for informal fire observation, we include some of them here with their historic brethren.

Within National Forest a number of old lookout sites are now within legislated National Forest Wilderness. Wilderness access is by foot or horse and I have given trail suggestions for visiting those sites. If there is no formal trail to the site within Wilderness I will give general directions.

The easiest lookouts to visit are those that can be reached by vehicle. I have listed "gravel road" as those unpaved roads that are generally in good shape and suitable for a family sedan, IF a "family sedan" actually exists today. You can substitute "SUV" for family sedan in my text and the translation will generally suffice. Quite simply, "gravel road" means the opportunity to acquire a little mud or dust on your travels and to experience the fabled "mud hole". Naturally, strong tires and good road clearance also help on gravel roads because mud puddles, seasonal washouts, blow down, stranded woodcutters parked in the middle of the road, and cut bank slumps are common. Many lookout access roads, shown on maps, can be a bit challenging and may not accommodate a sedan, particularly early in the summer when mud is prevalent and blow-down has not been cleared, or in the fall when early snow softens roads beyond civilized respectability. Dust is a subject for which I have no solution, other than "close your windows and turn on the AC!, the sound of birds is such a hindrance".

I have designated "four-wheel drive road or "4x4 jeep road" to indicate that you may require four-wheel drive, high clearance, and "jeep style" vehicles with very strong tires. Formal "Four-wheel driveways" are challenging for a four-wheel vehicle, equipped for challenges. Naturally, a four-wheel (4x4) drive road can also accommodate trail bike, mountain bike, hiker and horse. These roads may follow ridge routes that can be treacherous and rocky but are generally very scenic. Also, "un-wheeled" visitors will find that the vehicle traveling on treacherous roads are generally scarce and progressing "slow and easy" and therefore really don't conflict with the footed travelers. Still a good natured, respectable, and easy-going demeanor should always prevail when you are visiting public lands.

Travel and safety essentials (see Appendix C for further discussion): At remote locations visitors in the County are encouraged to carry the Five "10 Essentials" (sic) of forest recreation: 1.map and compass, 2. fire starter and matches, 3. jacket and hat, 4. extra water and food and 5. flashlight and cell phone. Visitors driving vehicles are additionally advised to carry a shovel, axe, and bucket as horse packers did in the old days. A cell phone is the new survival tool and most areas on the National Forest offer cell reception, but never count on it. Appendix C approaches essential survival gear from a variety of angles.

Anyone traveling dispersed or remote county locations is encouraged to carry toilet paper and a garden trowel for burying their human waste. Never assume that any toilet on the National Forest will be stocked with toiletries. Please pack out what you pack in, be careful with campfires, avoid harassing wildlife, and practice courtesy to other visitors; a broad statement which addresses barking dogs, loud music, and basic impoliteness which should be left at home. While traveling on forest roads, please drive slowly and yield to other traffic even if you have the right-of-way.

Several of these lookout points, though managed by firefighting agencies are located on privately owned land. A number of lookouts were placed and managed by the Yakama Tribe and you will have to find that information from the landowner or manager. Visit these privately managed sites only if you have specific permission to do so. There are no permits required to travel on National Forest Roads, BUT the State Department of Natural Resources (DNR), and State Department of Game (WDFW) require "state managed "discovery passes" for camping or parking. Some National Forest trailheads require a Trail Park Pass. Wilderness is closed to mechanical transport and large groups. Do not block campsites or access roads and do not leave valuables in your vehicle when wandering.

Benchmark (or Survey Caps) are the subject that fits nowhere else in this book, but everywhere. They are those 2" flat, canning jar size round brass or aluminum caps anchored in concrete or rock and embossed with elevations and site name. They give the lookout location validity and indicate the corresponding U.S.G.S. benchmark location found on maps. While looking for an abandoned lookout site, and no other evidence of the lookout remains, a final strategy would be to look for the benchmark in a prominent high point. Once you have found that, you are on your way to finding the other vanishing remains of your quest. Clover Springs Lookout site is a good example of a lookout with little remaining but the old, adjacent brass-cap benchmark.

Road access into and through the Tieton and Naches Basins

Just about every Lookout access route in this compendium begins in Yakima and originates from either White Pass Highway, known as U.S.12 OR Chinook Pass Highway State Route 410. In all subsequent references I will probably overlook who manages these routes and just refer to White Pass Highway or Chinook Pass Highway, or simply as Highway 12 or 410, as do the many flattened chipmunks who travel these routes from side to side instead of length wise, as cars normally do, and thus pay the cost not so much of traveling in the wrong direction but of traveling in half the wrong direction.

Chinook Pass Highway was opened across the Cascades at Chinook Pass in 1931 and is a seasonal highway today, closed due to snow from roughly Thanksgiving through May First, annually. An interesting historical photo dated 1923 seems to indicate that the Normile Grade up to the pass was already a travel feature, but that is all I know about that.

U. S. Highway 12, old State Route 5 (P.O. Star Route) didn't reach the Cascade Crest, at White Pass, until 1951. Before that all local alpine skiing concentrated at the American Ridge Ski Bowl near the mouth of Bumping Road. When the first skiers visited White Pass by car in the winter of 1951 and saw the depth and condition of the snow the fate of the Ski Bowl was set. Since that time the Ski Bowl Lodge and the multi-holed outhouse has served as a year around reservation recreation site .

Neither highway pass was built over existing trails, as was common in the history of pioneer pass highway routes. Instead, they were both located on long, even, southern grades, a tip of the hat to the advantages of sunshine in maintaining snow on roadways. Don't forget where history intercedes: The road crews began their work on White Pass near Sand Ridge Trailhead, thanks to the Bureau of Reclamation Clear Lake Dam Road, and the Chinook Pass efforts officially began on the east side at Morse Creek, thanks to earlier efforts of miners and such who resided near what is now the Timber Creek Summerhomes.

As long as we are talking about important dates in the development of roads and transportation in the Naches and Tieton Basins, this is a good time to mention the construction of the three Naches Basin irrigation reservoirs as they, along with mining roads, contributed and improved the first pioneer roadways up and into these basins. Bumping Lake was built in 1909 - 1910, the Clear Creek Dam was built in 1914 - 1915, and the Rimrock Reservoir was constructed in 1917 - 1925. We can assume that service roads for supplies and workers were built a year or two in advance of the start of construction. There is always a grandfather somewhere who claims to have driven White Pass Highway in 1950, which may have been possible, but it was an unfinished route under construction and not a general thoroughfare. SEE ALSO: Jumpoff Lookout #4 in this book for more local road development history.

TO THE READER: Notes of clarification

The fire lookout stations were called all sorts of things including Fire Lookout, Fire Watches, Forest Lookout, Watchtower, Lookout Stations, to name a few, but the lonely men and women who staffed those rustic old buildings were just called, "lookouts". It has been noted that bank robbers also use "Lookouts" to cover their retreat.

The popular **Pacific Crest National Scenic Trail** (PCNST), most often known as THE "Pacific Crest Trail" or "PCT" figures prominently throughout this book and my references to it will be reduced by at least a total page if I simply use the popular moniker "PCT", or in some cases "Crest Trail".

Travel Time: In an attempt to quantify the average travel time for the individual trips, from Yakima and back home there are so many variables that an accurate estimation is fruitless. Your travel time depends on how much "poking around" you do more than how many miles you plan to travel. Let it be said that most of these ventures can be taken, round trip, in a long day, including Tumac Mountain and Mount Aix. You can shorten that estimate by hurrying along or not stopping to gaze at every flower and photograph every mushroom. You can stretch out a trip by not getting in shape, by complaining to your travel companions, or by taking long naps. If you prefer your visit to Tumac Mountain or Mount Aix be leisurely, plan on camping. Leaving early is another approach, or leaving late. When Kristin and I climbed Desolation Peak on Ross Lake, it took us five tries, and after we finally got to the lookout we realized the practice trips were as interesting as the final conquest. Generally there is no competitive event associated with visiting lookouts: The final score is whatever you want it to be. Unplanned nights in the woods are usually uncomfortable and the result of poor planning.

To distinguish National **Legislated Wilderness** from the generic wilderness you get lost in your dreams, I have separated the two by the capital W for the legal kind. Yes, this may be out of order but how else to separate the two in any text or context as they are a bit different in important details.

Non-Wilderness Lookout Sites

Motorized access may be available

Be prepared for challenges

And expect some associated hiking

1

Blue Slide Lookout Site

6,785 Feet Elevation

T12N, R13E, Section 4

South of Divide Ridge west of Wiley City, WA

-ACCESS AT A GLANCE:

4X4 jeep trails on Divide Ridge, South of Rimrock Lake near the Wenatchee Forest boundary with bike and hiking opportunities.

- **Lookout Style/Year:** Older cupola building, 1946, or so to 1960 or so. Modern flattop building on 40' tower constructed 1961, removed around 1970.
- **Facilities Present:** Disappearing remains of kit garage.
- **Nearby Lookout and Observation Sites:** Darland Mountain Lookout, Site #11.
- **No Fire Lookout Panorama Photo on file.**
- **Difficulty getting to the lookout site** on a scale of 1 (easy) to 5 (difficult): **4**
- **Once there, difficulty to find the actual lookout remains** on a scale of 1 (easy) to 5 (difficult): **3**

Blue Slide lookout site is located at the crest of Short and Dirty Ridge, south and east of Rimrock Lake. The actual "Blue Slide" is a large (bluish) landslide tumbling into the South Fork Tieton River within the general vicinity of the old Blue Slide lookout or Gray Creek. Some historical tradition claims this slide was triggered in the late 1800s during an earthquake, but that rumor is unsubstantiated. Blue Slide lookout site is one of many high vistas along Divide Ridge. The view from Blue Slide is outstanding but getting there is challenging and requires sweat.

The most recent Blue Slide station was placed in 1961 and was similar in design to the existing Jumpoff Lookout station 10 miles to the Northeast along Divide Ridge. An older and smaller lookout station preceded that 14'x14' modern style, flat top building. The newer Blue Slide Station was used for only a few years and then abandoned. Unlike Jumpoff Lookout, this newer lookout was placed atop a 40 foot tower. The remains of Blue Slide were removed in 1970 after the guy wires and cabin were vandalized and the tower collapsed, no doubt assisted by wind. Not long ago the kit garage was still visible at the Lookout, but it too is fading with memory. In 1971 Bud Fisk, a past lookout was contracted to remove this station in its dilapidated condition and Youth Conservation Corp (YCC) crews worked on the rehabilitation of the site. Local residents who spent time on this site include Bud Fisk of Tieton and Terry Powell, long time resident of Trout Lodge, WA, a small nearby community along White Pass Highway also known to a few as Rimrock Retreat (which is the legal, plat designation).

SETTING: As you gaze to the north from the old lookout site you are viewing old sheep grazing areas where elk and deer now thrive. Clark's Nutcrackers, Ravens, and Mountain bluebirds all call this high ridge their natural home.

Short and Dirty Ridge is a long dusty ridge which seems well named. However, it was in fact named for a local sheepherder who ran his "Woollies" there before 1910. **Short and Dirty Cash** was a well-known shepherd in this area as well as on Bethel Ridge, where Cash Prairie is also named in his honor. It is conjectured that he was a man of short stature who bathed infrequently. In his defense, following 2,000 sheep around on dry ridges in late summer, not to

15

mention the scatological residue of those hungry "meadow maggots" was not conducive to cleanliness. There are no local sheepherders remembered as, "Short and Clean".

GETTING THERE

- (1) FROM Yakima through the Ahtanum Road system #1020
- BY WAY OF Darland Mt Lookout #11.

  (2) OR on foot FROM Rimrock Lake, hiking up the Short and Dirty Trail #1000-637.

Blue Slide offers one of the best views in the Naches Ranger District, sweeping over Pinegrass Ridge, into the upper Tieton South Fork and Goat Rocks, and into the Tieton Basin. However, it can only be visited by the most dedicated searcher for lookouts. Although the view is worth the effort this trip requires an adventurous spirit, a full day to explore, and the assistance of a good map. A narrow track, 4x4 driveway is the primary route to this rugged peak. Motorbikes, horseback riders, mountain bikers, or hikers can also visit this old lookout site along 4x4 routes, or pick up bits of the old single tread Short and Dirty trail that are still visible, filled in with the adjacent, climbing 4x4 route.

When Blue Slide Lookout was an active station the Forest Service crews from the Tieton Ranger Station serviced it by way of Tampico, west of Yakima through Wiley City. Oral tradition tells us that it required an entire day to drive up to the lookout and return to the old Tieton Ranger Station. The Ahtanum route is still the best way to visit Blue Slide, though hiking the old trail is more direct. This remote (and challenging) access may have been one of the reasons this site was eventually abandoned by 1971. Though you will want to take the ten essentials of survival for this trip, you will also want to be sure you have a proper map of the area before heading out. Much of the road trip from Wiley City is not on the Wenatchee

National Forest but the Naches Ranger District 1" topographic recreation map covers the western portion of this trip (See the South half of this double sided map).

(1) From the Ahtanum Road System: In a departure from straightforward directions, I'm going to offer unusual directions to Blue Slide. If you are going to drive to Blue Slide you might as well visit Darland Mt. also. If you are going to both, it is somewhat easier to go to Darland first, and then work your way back to Blue Slide on poorly signed and poorly mapped routes. With that in mind skip ahead to the directions for Darland Mt, #11, through Wiley City, Tampico, by the Ahtanum Guard Station and on to the Darland Mt. parking lot. From there you can follow the map as your legs and your vehicle are willing. Yes, this is the same Darland Mt. made famous in William O. Douglas *"Of Men and Mountains"* only Douglas liked to call it "Darling Mountain".

From Darland Mountain follow the 4x4 jeep Route #615 or other unmarked 4X4 spurs approximately 3 miles to the north toward Blue Lake. The old Blue Slide location has been removed from recent maps, but from Blue Lake you are looking on North for a short spur in the middle of section 4 (off Spur #615) with a mapped elevation of 6,785 feet at the spur end. If you somehow go on beyond this short spur, to the north you will come to the junction with the Short and Dirty 4x4 jeep Trail #637. In any case, your search will provide a unique setting and if you actually find the old lookout site you will be rewarded with great views.

(2) From Rimrock Lake: The most direct way to the lookout site is from the Tieton Basin, near Rimrock Lake, hiking or motorbiking along (up) the Short and Dirty Ridge: Turn off Hwy 12 west of Hause Creek campground on to paved Road #1200. Drive west to Rimrock Lake at the Peninsula and past the emergency airstrip, then south on the Tieton South Fork Road #1000. After one mile, turn left on spur road #1010 at Jay Hawk Flat and then right again in one mile on the #530 spur. Look for the unmarked four-wheel driveway trailhead on the left and park well off the road. Fourwheel (jeep) driveways over Short and Dirty Ridge as well as the 4x4 jeep trails that drop from Divide Ridge into the Tieton South Fork are a mess with massive erosion, mud, and very steep, unsafe side hills. Because travelers have died on these trails I am not suggesting them for any type of wheeled travel, uphill or downhill. IF you must brave this route with a vehicle, walk the steepest routes first to assess the situation and evaluate your experience level.

SEE ALSO

- Darland Mountain Lookout #11, this book

2

Devil's Slide Overlook Site

5,525 Feet Elevation

T17N, R15E, Section 17

Spring Creek and Milk Creek Basins

- ACCESS AT A GLANCE:

State Route Highway 410 Near Whistlin' Jack Lodge.
Hike in from either of two trailheads off Forest Service gravel roads.
- **Lookout Style/Year:** Pole platform style "crow's nest"
occasional site use in conjunction with (Big) Bald Lookout, #9 this book
utilized sometime in the past to some later time in the past.
- **Facilities Present:** None.
- **Nearby Lookout and Observation Sites**: Big Bald Mt. Lookout #9.
- **No Fire Lookout Panorama Photograph on record, as would be expected**
- **Difficulty getting to the lookout site** on a scale of 1 (easy) to 5 (difficult): **2**
- **Once there, difficulty to find the actual lookout remains** on a scale of 1 (easy) to 5 (difficult): **5**

Although Devil's Slide is an interesting geological feature and its rim offers an outstanding view of the lower Naches Basin, the large namesake slide never hosted an actual lookout station. Devil's Slide observation point was simply a tent and firefinder

19

placed on some sort of primitive stand, sometimes called a "Crows Nest", used in conjunction with the nearby Bald Mt. Lookout. A "Crow's Nest" lookout site can be as simple as a platform or com-plicated as a perch constructed in the top of a tree, accessed by some sort of ladder.

This observation spot brings up an interesting issue: the Forest Service field crews knew many good viewpoints throughout the district, and used them to locate elusive smokes. Crow's Nest type lookouts are often overlooked on lookout lists as firefighters used just about any perch with a good view to better detect forest fires. There were numerous "Viewpoints" similar to **Devil's Slide** around the forest that early rangers used in conjunction with actual lookouts, either to search for smokes or simply to enjoy lunch. You'll always see the surrounding topography in a fresh light when you "look things over" from a higher perspective.

The exact location of the old observation site is now forgotten, but it must have been one of the promontories along Devil's Slide Ridge, as it climbs toward Bald Mt. If someone visits one of those view points and notices some old rusty nails or other possible remains, be sure to record the GPS location and contact any of the number of Lookout Location books or web sites. Discovering this site will assure that your name will go down in history along with any books, novels, or movies made about this old site.

If you spot Mt. Goats on this visit, please observe at a distance and avoid stressing them by crowding. The easy way to do this is to imagine finding a wild goat in YOUR home.

SETTING

I remember working as a Wilderness Ranger and receiving radioed instructions to climb a nearby high point to "take a look" And seldom did I casually visit a high point, such as McNeil Peak, Shellrock Peak, Burnt Mt, Iron Stone Mt, Bismarck Peak, and others without taking the time to make sure there wasn't' a "sleeper" fire, resting in a snag or stump, just starting to send up a smoke column. It is worth noting that in the week after a "lightening bust", a dry windy day would usually awaken sleeping embers and on those days all the field crews were weary and prone to gazing at the forest for the first tale-tell sign of smoke. Smokey Bear merely "sniffed the air" which also works.

Another forgotten aspect of fire location was the status at the ranger station for those who were skilled at "turning in a smoke", particularly if you were the first to locate a fire which eventually grew to legendary status. Whenever crews talked about a particularly memorable fire someone would usually say, "Didn't Mike Hiler first call in that fire from McNeil Peak" or some such. Of course lookouts, being trained to recognize smokes early, like to play that game or should I say, "we were required to". Even today I find myself just naturally noticing the color of smoke and muttering to anyone who will listen, "Must be a structure fire, see the black smoke". And, as they say of Smokey, "He could find a fire before it started to flame", that's why they call him Smokey, that was how he got his name"!

No date is assigned to the use of Devil's Slide (or Devil's Table) Viewpoints, and no panorama photos are on record. Earl Coleman Brown, Lookout Artist, rendered his drawing of Devil's Table from verbal descriptions of older Forest Service friends who remembered it. Packy Howett, Bald Mt. Lookout of note surely visited these sites in the 1930s.

GETTING THERE

Devil's Slide is an old and very large landslide in upper Milk Creek, east of the Little Naches Basin. It's extend is apparent on any topological map. Access to the Devil's Slide is via the **closed** Gold Creek Road #1703 accessed from the Spring Creek Road

#1705 near Whistlin' Jack Lodge off Highway 410 east of the Little Naches #1900 Road. Or, you can drop into the slide from Big Bald Mt the same day you conquer Big Bald Lookout # 9.

- (1) FROM Hwy 410 near Whistlin' Jack Lodge, drive the Spring Creek Road #1705
  - to the Gold Creek Road #1703 and on to an informal trailhead at Gold Creek Road end.
  - Spring Creek Road is generally in very good shape and this is probably the best route
  - anyway. The upper sections of this route offer outstanding views and I recommend
  - it even if you aren't going to hike up to the trail along Devil's Slide Ridge to Big Bald
  - Lookout. Hike up on Trail #966 from this informal trailhead.
- (2) OR FROM Highway 410 Drive the Gold Creek Road #1703 to the road end
  - **though the Gold Creek Road is often washed out** at Gold Creek crossing
  - and option #1 above is probably the only possible vehicle route anyway.
- (3) OR FROM near Bald Mt #9, hiking down on Trail #966 by way of 4x4 jeep route #644.

Final Thought: Devil's Slide is often mixed up with Devil's Table, over in the Rattlesnake drainage, near its' geological partner, Meeks Table. Both may or may not have had some sort of informal viewing platform and no doubt fires were called in from both locations. I'll leave Devil's Table to the adventurous who likes to find something not on the map.

SEE ALSO

- Big Bald Mt Lookout

- Campbell, Newell: *The Geology of Yakima*

3

Edgar Rock Lookout Site

3,620 Feet Elevation or some other similar elevation

T17N, R14E, Section 26

Overlooking Highway 410 near Whistlin' Jack Lodge

- ACCESS AT A GLANCE:

Off Highway 410, Forest roads near Whistlin' Jacks Lodge **and then** hike in from either of two trailheads off Forest Service roads.

- **Lookout Style/Year:** Older lookout style cabin 1934. Removed 1951.
- **Facilities Present:** Foundation corners and remarkable view.
- **Nearby Lookout and Observation Sites:** Little Bald site #5 and garage.
- **Fire Lookout Panorama Photo date:** 1934.
- **Difficulty getting to the lookout site** on a scale of 1 (easy) to 5 (difficult): **3**
- **Once there, difficulty to find the actual lookout remains** on a scale of 1 (easy) to 5 (difficult): **2**

L ittle information remains on this overlook. Gretta Gossett, in her book *Beyond the Bend* mentions that Edgar Rock Lookout was used for "weekend occupancy". The point on which the old station was built is a unique rocky outcrop that allows great views up and down the upper Naches River. It was built here for easy access to the Ranger Station, for a quick response during dry periods of the summer, and when smoke was in the air or a summer thunderstorm threatened.

The old Edgar lookout site has almost returned to the natural condition and the view from that promontory reminds us why it was once an important part of the fire detection system for the Naches District, particularly after recreation campers started frequenting the basin.

At a comparatively low elevation the view does not match those of higher stations, but it does give an unexpected and dynamic view of the surroundings, including Cleman Mt and connected drainage openings, a remarkable peek up the Little Naches toward Government Meadows, and a birds-eye view of .the small mountain community of Cliffdell, which has a unique place in local geology, as well as Washington state pioneer history.

Some bits and pieces of the Edgar Rock Lookout building remain to remind us of the lookouts who worked there, including Dave Wright (1937) of Yakima. At one time, there were many of these "quick access" observation sites backing up the network of regular, and more remote lookouts. Be sure to take your camera on this visit. See Pyramid Peak #13 for more of this Naches pioneer history.

SETTING

The Old Naches Pass Trail once followed the Naches River through what is now Cliffdell. The old trail likely traversed the south side of the Naches River, directly across from present day Whistlin' Jack Lodge, a popular lodge located in the heart of the Cliffdell mountain community. The pioneer trail was used by the Wilkes "Pacific Exploration Expedition" of 1841. The Longmire Wagon Train passed near here, heading to western Washington in the fall of 1853.

Theodore Winthrop almost surely passed within a few feet of what is now Whistlin' Jack Lodge in 1853 when he cut a swath through the Oregon Territory, abusing the trust of local natives. His book, *Canoe and Saddle* was popular during the civil war and has remained in print ever since. In those frontier days the trail was simply a "blazed travelway or primitive stock driveway unlike today's established roads or numbered trails. Old maps indicated that the trail corridor passed near the present location of the Crag summerhomes.

In the fall of 1853 a singular historical event occurred near Cliffdell resulting in the naming of Edgar Rock. That year Army Scout **John Edgar** was riding ahead of a military detachment lead by Col. Wright. Wright and his solders were heading for Naches Pass from their station at Fort Steilacoom. In the vicinity of Sawmill Flat (according to Gossett), Edgar encountered the scouts for a group of natives resolved to greet the military with force. Edgar, who was married to a Yakama woman, learned of the war party's intent and returned to the military group with the news. They fled back to Steilacoom, to resume the war at a more opportune time. Edgar Rock, a remnant of an old volcano, was named in memory of Edgar after he died in the Yakima Indian War three years later. Jo Miles' fascinating book about those times, ***Kamiakin Country*** details the entire episode with more clarity.

Cliffdell is a very apt name for this small mountain community as it is both "cliffy" and located in a parklike setting. However, it was actually named for **Clifford and Della Schott** onetime residents. Earlier names may have been (to some) "Spring Hill", not to be confused with the alluvial "Spring Hill" one mile east of Trout Lodge on the Tieton side. Some private land exists here but other cabins are permitted on National Forest ownership. These permit holders own their cabins but pay an annual fee to the Forest Service for land use. Through roundabout government accounting methods, which no one actually understands, the special use receipts are returned to local county road and school funds. In return, the summerhome owners are generally abused by the Forest Service in due course.

Although this book is about Lookouts I'd be derelict if I didn't mention that in 1894 or so, near about Boulder Cave, local resident Barney Moore killed the last **bald faced bear** in the area, or so part of the Gretta Gossett story goes. Moore was not prosecuted for the wonton slaughter of an animal that probably forgot to shave and may or may not have had large feet as is anyone's guess.

A final bit of information concerns the River Meadows along the Old River Road in the vicinity of the Edgar Rock Trailhead. This was once the Fontaine Ranch and the old ranch house is still a prominent feature of the Fontaine area. That large house size boulder in the meadow appeared one morning as Mr. Fontaine was preparing to milk his cows.

GETTING THERE

- (1) FROM Naches Old River Road #1704-311
  Trail #964 to #964-A near Lost Creek Village.

- (2) OR TO the end of Road #1761 and a lower junction
  of Trail #964 in section 34

  AND then on down the hill toward the lookout on unmarked Trail #964,

  TO Trail #964-A and on to the Lookout after wondering a bit.

- (3) OR FROM Road #1706 off Highway 410 near
  Cliffdell, to the Junction with Trail #964.

There are two general ways to hike to Edgar Rock: one on a climbing trail from near Lost Creek Village and the other is hiking down an unmarked trail from the road systems above. Up or down, take a map.

(1) The Trail #964 is a relatively steep climb but this route offers the advantage of being a bit easier to find the lookout. Near Gold Run (Highway 410 near Cliffdell) turn onto Road #1704 and drive into the Fontaine community on the "Old River Road". Turn left just before reentering the National Forest on Road #1704-311, 0.8 mile toward Lost Creek Village. The trailhead for Trail #964 should be marked. If not, watch for a road switchback/wide spot on the right with evidence of trailhead parking. Take a good look around for orientation before you depart to the lookout as **Haystack Rock** will be a main attraction and the landmark to guide you on this hike. It's one of those landmarks that doesn't need a description even if you've never seen an unbaled haystack. The round trip takes approximately three hours so allow extra time for photos or sight-seeing.

Climb toward Edgar Rock on Trail #964 to Trail #964-A (on the right) and it will lead you to the old lookout. The hike climbs almost 800 vertical feet over the two mile trip. The views are outstanding. The unmarked condition of the trail makes it a perfect seek and find experience for those who love the challenge.

(2) The easier route is downhill from the end of Road #1761 at an informal trail crossing, Section 34. Approach the peak f61m the upper road system by way of State Route 410 at the Boulder Cave (Camp Roganunda) turnoff, one mile west to Whistlin' Jack Lodge. Cross the Naches River, turn right on Road #1704 and drive a short distance to Road #1706 on the left, and on up to Road #1761 on the left. At the end of road you may see a portion of the upper Lost Creek Trail #964 sign pointing the way down toward the Edgar Rock Trail #964-A junction. The trailhead is primitive but plenty of good parking and some dispersed camping is available. The trail itself is a bit hidden and if you can't find the single tread, follow the jeep road down the hill a few hundred (horizontal) yards and watch for the trail to cross the 4x4 jeep road at old signage around three miles further on the left, or what seems reasonable by following the map. All things considered you'll get there. The trail follows another ¼ mile and connects where the "A" Trail branches off toward the lookout.

(3) If you want a simpler, but higher approach, simply stay on Road #1706 to the trail beginning on the left. It should be but may not be signed, or you can feel it out based on where cars have been camping and turning around.

A detailed map, such as the Naches Ranger District One inch to the mile topographic recreation and fireman's map is invaluable here, but you can follow road numbers to get to the trailhead or to just generally get lost. Using your 1" map and a bit of creative sleuthing, follow an unmarked trail downhill, looking all the while for signs of an informal trail (trail signs thrown in the brush, tree blazes, gum wrappers). Eventually you will stumble onto Trail #964 which you will follow on down the hill to trail #964A on the left which will lead you to the lookout site where your "Am I lost?" concerns will vanish.

Yes, this particular lookout site offers an opportunity to get temporarily lost but most of the time you can see a portion of cars traveling east and west on Chinook Pass Highway, and if evening approaches, just hike downhill and be saved by the plucky Camp Roganunda campers

SEE ALSO

- *Edgar Rock* a free Forest Service handout, Naches Ranger Station
- Winthrop, Theodore: *Canoe and Saddle*
- Miles, Jo: *Kamiakin Country*, Caxton Press, 2017
- Little Bald Lookout, #5
- Clover Springs Lookout, #18

- Gossett, Gretta: *Beyond the Bend.* A discussion on John Edgar and

  W. W. de Lacy, Adjunct to Col Shaw, p. 466 and Cliffdell comments, p.462

- Gossett, GrettA: the *"Bald Faced Bear"* story, p. 111

- Cyr, Suzy: *Tanum, The story of Bumping Lake"*, 2022

4

Jumpoff Lookout Station

5,745 Feet Elevation (among other similar estimates)

T13N, R14E, Section 1

(see the boundary between Sections 2 and 3, Metzkers Map binder, 1934)

West of Tieton City overlooking the Tieton Basin to the West

ACCESS AT A GLANCE:

- 4X4 jeep type access on 13 mile unmaintained Forest Service gravel road,
- OR hike from Long Lake Trailhead, OR bushwhack from road ends.

- **Lookout Style/Year:** Older Lookout style cupola: 1930's – 1958,
>   - Newer flat top style 1961 to the Present.
>   - Garage removed 1975 before it was eligible for historic protection.

- **Facilities Present:** Last surviving Lookout Station in Yakima Co.

- **Nearby Lookout and Observation Sites:** Windy Point Overlook 2 miles up road #1302
>   Access to and outstanding views of Kloochman Rock from Road #1200-570, Kloochman
>   Rock Peak a somewhat technical climb, and Goose Egg Peak from Rimrock Peninsula.

31

- Fire Lookout Panorama Photo date: 1929.

- Difficulty getting to the lookout site on a scale of 1 (easy) to 5 (difficult): **4**

- Once there, difficulty to find the actual lookout remains on a scale of 1 (easy) to 5 (difficult): **0**

Jumpoff Lookout is one of the best known fire guard lookouts in the Naches Basin, probably because it still exists. (See disclaimer at end of Jumpoff chapter) Locally known as "Jumpoff Joe", though technically "Jumpoff Joe" is a lookout located near Detroit, Oregon. But whatever the name, this point offers a beautiful, though some-times challenging, thirteen mile (dead end) drive through open sage, shrub steppe, infinitely rocky ridge top, stretching from the Tieton River at Windy Point floor through Gerry Oak and pine forests and ending at a remarkable view directly into the Tieton Basin. View-ing to the west you will look down over Kloochman Rock, Goose Egg Mountain, Westfall Rock, Rimrock Lake, Lost Lake, Jumpoff Meadow, and Heaven.

Jumpoff is the last remaining lookout station in the Naches District for a number of reasons. This site is a ragged basalt point with sheer sides to the east, north, and west and offers excellent views into the Tieton Basin with reasonable coverage for the ridges of Oak Creek and Bear Canyon. Probably as important as the view was the weather station status and relatively central radio relay location, as Jumpoff monitored the Old Tieton Ranger District's radio traffic during summer months. With road access, good views of Divide Ridge lightning storms, and relatively light snowpack for its elevation, it served the Forest Service well into the air patrol era.

The present Jumpoff Lookout Station is of the modern design, constructed at the same time as the now departed Blue Slide Lookout, site #1 in this book. The older Jumpoff building, a two story stone and wood building sat just south of the present building with the cupola placed over the living quarter. A spring, once used by lookouts, is located 100 yards southeast of the present station, and the old phone line to the Ranger Station went directly north and west down the knife ridge to Jumpoff Meadow below. Dry site, dispersed camping is available at several areas along the Jumpoff road near the Lookout.

A kit garage once stood south of the building but was removed in the 1970's and the old outhouse was replaced in the late 1970's with one of modern design but it "bit the dust" as well, probably owing to the steady wind and annual snowpack. A monument is placed near the lookout in 1987, to commemorate Kevin Miller, a popular and dedicated watcher at this station for a number of years. A large accumulation of debris is evident on the rocks below the site to the east, a tribute to the old style of tin can recycling utilizing rust and time in equal proportions. Oh yea, I stumbled over the fact that Jeff McLain constructed Jumpoff, I'm just not sure which Jumpoff he built, the new one or the old one?

Past lookouts at this station include Mike Hiler (69 – 73), Audrey Dunnington (60 – 68), Louie Van Hoy (37 - 41), Arvel Willard (1942) and Keith Matson (1943). Modern lookouts include "Octavio", Kevin Miller, Jennifer Townsend, Leslie and her acrobatic boy friend Poncho, and others.

SETTING

Local history intersects your visit here in a number of ways. Between highway 12 and the first viewpoint two miles up Road #1302 (see Windy Point overlook below) you will cross over the Yakima Tieton Canal as it flows through the mile long **Trail Creek Tunnel** below you. You may have seen the old canal phone line corridor following the tunnel route overland. A spur road to the left, about a mile up Road #1302, now closed, drops back East to the canal and dead ends at a maintenance point further down the canal.

This Trail Creek Tunnel was named after an old trail accessing the river at Windy Point from the south ridge-top travel route used by basin natives and pioneers to get to and from the Tieton Basin. In those days, travel along the river was practically impossible due to underbrush but river access was desirable because that was where the fish were.

From the (two mile) overlook a big switchback turns back west. Your trip for the next 11 miles will be a winding ridgetop climb to Jumpoff Point at 5,745 feet elevation. About half way up, the Hatton route (historic wagon road) junction turns back east to the town of Tieton, a small fruit community discovered and rebuilt in the 2000s by Yuppie artists. Hatton Road, no doubt the Historic route to the west end of Jumpoff Ridge, is the proposed William O. Douglas Trail, but private sections now obstruct travel.

John Russell, Tieton Basin pioneer and railroad survey packer ferried supplies along this Jumpoff Ridge route from Yakima to his Tieton Basin ranch as early as 1890. He packed butter (his cash crop) to town, traveling at night to keep the butter cool. Russell drove a wagon to a point near Jumpoff, disassembled it, and packed it in on horseback to his ranch in what is now the bottom of upper Rimrock Lake, near Russell Creek.

Later, as early as 1910, the Tieton Cattleman's Association drove their herds from Tieton City toward the Tieton Basin along this route and "dropped" them into the basin near Louie Gap. **Homer Splawn**, son of Jack and Margret Larson Splawn, remembered driving cattle over the ridge when he was but a strapling. His memory was riding his horse to the edge of the incline, pulling back on the reigns, and sliding a ways down the slope as he helped "punch" cattle into the basin, sometime in his past.

Many outstanding views are on display along the 13 mile Jumpoff Road #1302. Be on the lookout for old cabins on the south side of the Jumpoff Road. An old saw mill foundation is on a faint road to the north. When you cross under a power line, follow it (on foot) to the **Sentinel Creek Overlook.** As you view down the power line into the Trout Lodge settlement below, look across the Tieton Canyon to the north for the best view of the very old **Ancient Tieton Volcano**, an ancient rising of stone now almost obscured by time. It is probably appropriate to call that volcano older than dirt. Two million years ago, give or take a few, this stone mass was as high as Mt. Rainier and a million years ago it was as high as Goat Rocks (the lower snow covered peaks to the west). Will Goat Rocks look like this in a million years and will Mt. Rainier look like this in two million? Geologists are consistently vague on this point. We will have to wait and see.

Looking west toward Westfall Rock and on up Rimrock Lake to the west, Highway 12 winds toward White Pass, just visible on the westward ridge. The Highway 12 tunnel at Westfall Rock was not cut until 1936 and White Pass, named for a Railroad Surveyor, fortunately for the ski area named White, breached the Cascades by highway in 1951. Rimrock Reservoir is held back by the Tieton Dam, a structure once the highest earth filled dam in the world. In 1925 it was christened, fittingly, with apple juice, as this reservoir is part of the Yakima impoundment system which makes the Yakima Valley fruit industry possible. The debt for the irrigation canal was long sense repaid by irrigation farmers, and the success of this government project is now a calling card for government interference on all levels, if not strident socialism, though those debates have long since been shipped out of the valley in apple boxes. Also, as you pass the Tieton Dam do not forget that the largest Bull Trout in the Washington State universe, locally called a "Dolly Varden" and weighing 22.5 pounds, was angled in the dam plunge pool in 1961. See introduction page "page 9", this book for more ramblings on local road history.

GETTING THERE

- (1) FROM Windy Point : Forest access Road #1302, 13 miles.

- (2) OR FROM Long Lake by way of Louie Gap 4x4 Way #1126
- by way of paved Forest Road #1201 off the Tieton Road #1200.
- (3) OR the more interesting access to Long Lake
- by way of Chimney Peaks Road #1200-570 shortcut.
- (4) OR cross-country FROM the end of Forest Road #1201-569 over game trails,
- following your map with an eye to the lookout up there on the ridge.

I suggest one of three ways to get to the Lookout: (1) Driving the old Jumpoff Road #1302, now a challenging 4x4 jeep route, (2) Hiking in from Long Lake over the Divide Ridge Trail, by way of Louie (Van Hoey) Gap jeep trail from Long Lake, and (3) Bushwhacking along informal game trails using GPS coordinates from the end of Forest Road #1201–569.

(1) **4x4 Forest jeep Road #1302 departs Highway 12** between the Windy Point Bridges and climbs several miles to the top of Jumpoff Ridge, also known as the south end of the Divide Ridge. The first three or four miles of this route is suitable for some cars and most trucks, but the road gets progressively worse at the mid-way point (6 miles). From here it requires strong tires, good road clearance, and the extra advantage of four-wheel-drive. At about 10 miles it becomes a rocky, rutted mess which may even turn back 4x4 vehicles but the hike is stunning and as long as you stay on top the ridge, there is little opportunity to get lost.

At around the 2 mile point the scenery opens, the road makes a westward turning switchback and follows the ridge westward for another 10 miles. At this point Jumpoff is in the distant view to the west. A few hundred feet to the northeast of this 2 mile ridgetop switch back a remarkable observation point gives views down into the Tieton Canyon and across the canyon over toward Oak Creek to the North. From this point on west motorhomes and trailers are not recommended.

This overlook at the two mile point is also unique because it is one of the few places in the valley where you can view the top of large basalt crystals, those (cow?) pie shaped rosettes protruding up through the soil. Look at these rough, flat shape rocks and leave them in place for others to enjoy.

From here the road gets progressively rougher as you travel west along the ridge top. About half way to the lookout (6 or 7 miles) you will drive under a power line, crossing to Trout Lodge. The drop-off of this power line down into the basin is also a great view to the northwest, and the power line gives map followers a point of reference as it is clearly marked on the 1" to the mile Forest Service field map.

As you progress west you will play hide and seek with the lookout, sporadically visible throughout the trip. Eventually, you'll drive over a cattle guard, marked on your map as a Forest Service Boundary. This cattle guard is a reminder of the open range cattle grazing permits of yesteryear. Here, the road climbs out of the rock zone into the "wash out" mud zone, bops over a peak, and drops the last mile to the lookout. There is some good, dry, camping in this last two miles. The clear night sky, the smells of the sage, and the singing of the coyotes should remind you where you are, the cow poop is a bonus. If a domestic cow greets you in the morning, she is just curious. Springs and water spigots are rare and if you plan to camp, bring your own water.

A word of caution about this 13 mile dead end route: Blowdown (trees) is common, mud is expected the last few miles, strong tires are required. Until July 1 a snowbank often blocks a portion of the upper road. One idea is to park wherever your vehicle complains and then walk or Mt. Bike on up the ridge, remembering that if you stop at the three mile mark, you have an 18 mile, unassisted round trip hike ahead of you. One consistent aspect of the Jumpoff Road is that the further you go, the worse the road gets and the better the view.

> **(2) Hiking in from Long Lake by way of Louie Way Gap:** Turn off highway 12 near Hause Creek Campground onto paved county Road #1200. You can drive up toward Long Lake either on the #1201 Road, on past Camp Ghormley OR stay on the paved #1200 Road a-ways, turning off on the Chimney Peaks#1200-570 spur, a ways before the Tieton Emergency Landing Strip where Goose Egg cliffs are prominent on the north side of the Road #1200.

The Chimney Peak Road spur "short-cut" #1200-570 takes you right up through **Chimney Peaks**, worthy of photos, but not safe to climb. This shortcut is the preferred route with better scenery, less traffic, dispersed camping, and no asphalt chuckholes. Turn right at the #1201 junction near Lost Lake and progress to Long Lake

As you drive "ON UP" to Long Lake you will get good views of **Kloochman Rock** THE very old basalt dike projecting into the Tieton Sky. If you wish to explore the base of Kloochman you can find nearby parking turnouts. This monolith is not suitable for technical climbing and free climbing can be arduous or even dangerous. If you are inclined, to climb, read the last Chapter of William O. Douglas *Of Men and Mountains*.

On to Jumpoff Lookout from the Long Lake trailhead: Louie Gap 4x4 jeep Way #613, the first segment of this hike, departs from Forest Road #1201 at Long Lake. At the Long Lake trailhead you will find shady camping or parking, through early summer, mosquitoes may be mistaken for angry badgers. Walk to and around the lake, and connect with the 4x4 route to the east. From here the jeep route parallels the old single tread trail, either road to trail will take you up to **Louie Gap Way**, named for Louie Van Hoey, early Jumpoff Lookout. The only certified wild badger I have ever seen in Washington state was near here. Before he departed he glanced toward me for a second with a look that could kill.

At Long Lake you will encounter a unique bit of history in the form of a very old "Adirondack" type trail shelter, constructed by the Civil Conservation Corps (CCC). Hard to believe one of those shelters still survives and is in such good shape, owing no doubt to the cedar roof and to some past love and care by way of the many fishermen, hikers, and campers who have visited this spot.

At the gap (or pass) the single tread portion of the trail crosses the Divide Ridge Trail. A right turn will take you to the top of Divide Ridge, to the west and on to Dome Peak and Darland Mountain Lookout, but save that for another day and turn left to follow the east segment on up to Jumpoff. In less than a mile the 4x4 way will fade to an unmarked single tread trail, you will break out of the trees and onto a long, bare, rocky slope. Near bench mark SB 1146 you will continue to traverse to an informal road system to the top leading to Jumpoff Road #1302. Veer northwest along the ridge and the Lookout will quickly jump into view.

(3) **Cross country bushwhacking:** The GPS route requires driving to the end of forest Road #1201- 569 or the end one of the many roads just about anywhere in this area and following your coordinates up to the lookout. Old maps of this area strongly suggest an alternative to Louie Gap trail, an east-west trail branching west off the Jumpoff Road, seemingly headed for Jump off Meadow. Several historians are working on this historic trail location; stay tuned for further developments. And don't forget, this particular trail location is part of the planned William O. Douglas Trail, stretching from Yakima west.

OTHER VIEWS TO CONSIDER

Windy Point Overlook: Windy Point overlook is the stunning view two miles up the #1301 Road from Highway 12. At the first ridge top switchback park and wander up to the point a few hundred feet to the northeast.

Kloochman Rock (and Chinney Peaks): Kloochman Rock, made famous by the chapter in the William O. Douglas book, *Of Men and Mountains* is almost mythical in its statuesque splendor. If you use the Long Lake to Louie Gap route to get to Jumpoff, as I mention in the above # 2 alternate route, I suggest you use the paved Forest Road #1200-570 spur route towards Lost Lake, passing Chimney Peaks on the way up and then onto the #1201 Road near Long Lake. The Kloochman Rock trailhead is a mile or two on up #1201 on the left with a good view of the south end of Kloochman on your right.

Goose Egg Peak: in full view from Jumpoff, looking to the West, Goose Egg also offers great views for anyone wanting go hike up a steep user trail for a gain of almost 2,000 vertical feet. The unmarked trail starts near the Rimrock Boat Launch parking lot on Rimrock Peninsula.

Safety Note: Jumpoff Lookout sits on a basalt bedrock cliff on the east and west, with a steep spine dropping dangerously to the North, thus the name. There are no guard rails at the lookout so if you drive, park your vehicle carefully or better yet, park at the last, shady switchback (site of an old camp) and walk the last 100 yards.

> **DISCLAIMER: As we go to press** Jumpoff Lookout has acquired a new 80 foot ATT cell phone tower in its' south yard. The points in favor of such an unlikely addition to the site are sketchy at best and the project managers may eventually realize there are better unique Historical Register view points to impact. If the lookout station has vanished when you get there, read the preceding sketch as history

and enjoy the view! Perhaps ATT's maintenance crew will contribute some badly needed maintenance to the access road or install needed signage.

SEE ALSO

- Jumpoff Informational Handout, Naches Ranger Station.
- US Weather records for Jumpoff: site "052-302", online.
- Hiler, Mike. *Buckskin Larch and Bedrock*, Cave Moon Press, 2011: Lookout poems based on Jumpoff Lookout. See bibliography of this book.
- Hiler, Mike. *Lookout Stories* this book.
- *Douglas, William O.: Of Men and Mountains* for his chapter about Kloochman Rock.

5

Little Bald Mountain Lookout Site

6,108 Feet Elevation

T16N, R13E, Section 2

East of Goose Prairie, WA on the Clover Springs Road

- ACCESS AT A GLANCE:

Generally maintained Forest Service roads
from multiple points off Highway 410 near Whistlin'
Jack Lodge. May be challenging in places but suitable for
hiking or mountain bike.

- **Lookout Style/Year:** Older style on 30' tower completed 1936, burned by accident 1980.
- **Facilities Present:** Concrete tower foundation and kit garage managed by volunteers.
- **Nearby Lookout and Observation Sites:** Clover Springs lookout Site #18

and Edgar Rock Lookout site #3.
- **Fire Lookout Panorama Photo date:** 1934.
- **Difficulty getting to the lookout site** on a scale of 1 (easy) to 5 (difficult): **4**
- **Once there, difficulty to find the actual lookout remains** on a scale of 1 (easy) to 5 (difficult): **2**

Little Bald Mountain rises from the mouth of Bumping River toward Nelson Ridge. It affords an outstanding view into the lower Bumping Basin and down the Naches River toward Rattlesnake Creek. This lookout site is accessible with a sedan (with good tires), though the site is somewhat remote and the road can be rocky, muddy or rutted in season.

Little Bald Lookout was constructed in 1936 (Gretta Gossett) and rebuilt sometime later. The garage and older toilet were placed in 1934. Little Bald was a very serviceable lookout for the old Naches District. When the modern tower was burned accidentally in 1980, it was the last remaining lookout in the old Naches District. Little Bald offered good, central radio monitoring for the District, overlooked a sizeable piece of lower elevation ground, and monitored much of the District's recreation areas.

The lookout tower footings remain as foundation for a modern radio relay facility and the kit garage with adjacent outhouse, maintained by volunteers, is still being used responsibly by the public. Some old railings remain to prevent visitors from driving over the ridge into oblivion near-by. Park carefully and scan this unique view. From here you can see back toward (and over) the Yakima City area, as well as to the west and north. A topographic map will help your orientation from this point.

A number of Yakima residents spent time working on the Little Bald Station. Marion Hessey worked here during World War II (reporting to Horace Cooper and Charles Johnson), and a lady named Rose worked there during most of the 1940s through 1954.

SETTING

The Little Bald companion fire observatory was Clover Springs (lookout # 18), offering an alternative viewpoint that is accessible from Little Bald. The view from Clover Springs is to the west overlooking the upper North Fork Rattlesnake basin now mostly within Wilderness. While Little Bald Lookout at 6,108 feet elevation was situated on top of a 30 foot tower, the Clover Springs Lookout was a ground level platform crow's nest providing simple shelter of some sort? Little Bald had a commanding view and was a primary station which lookouts occupied the entire summer.

The Nile Flats area, along Road #1600, is a popular camping and hunting area once housing the Nile Box Mill. Around 1930 the Orr family operated a pine box mill here, strangely called, **The Nile Box Mill.** Huge old Growth pine logs were skidded down to the mill over a rough skidway, pulled by solid rubber tired vehicles. Later known as the Nile Railroad, this was simply a hauling skid powered by surplus World War I vehicles. At one time a number of loggers and millers worked and lived here. The **Little Fish Ranger Station** was located here and the earliest 932nd Company Civil Conservation Corps (CCC) Camp was located here during its first year of operation before moving to Current Flats. A YMCA boys camp also occupied a site here for a while during the 1920s - 1930).

For more "Setting" read ahead to the Clover Springs Lookout section as I combined most of the lore of this area in that scree.

GETTING THERE

- (1) FROM Cliffdell: FS Road #1706 to #1600 to Spur #231.

- (2) FROM the Nile, Road #1600 off Highway 410 at the Woodshed Restaurant

- through Nile Flats and on to Spur #231.

- (3) FROM Halfway Flats: Forest Road #1600 by way of Forest Road #1706

- By way of Road #1709 at Halfway Flats.

- (4) OR HIKE FROM Half Way Flats on Trail #961 to Saddle Camp and beyond.

There are several ways to get to the Little Bald Road access Spur #1706-231 turnoff, ½ mile from the lookout. They are (1) From Cliffdell on Road #1706 to the Road #1600, (2) Through the Nile Flats, Road #1600, (3) From Halfway Flats on Road #1709 to Road # 1706 and on to Road #1600, (4) From Halfway Flats on the Half Way Flats Trail #961, and (5) returning to Highway 410 from Clover Springs you can wind down toward Cliffdell and stop to inspect the **old CCC picnic shelter at Boulder Cave.**

(1) From Cliffdell

The most direct route is driving from Cliffdell. Heading west on Highway 410 a mile west of Whistlin' Jacks Lodge turn left onto Forest Road #1706 and cross the Naches River toward **Camp Roganunda** and **Boulder Cave.** Stay on Road #1706 up the hill and continue on for 7 miles to the #1600 Road. Around 2 miles beyond the turn off onto #1600 you will see the Little Bald Spur #231 on the right.

Road conditions in the Devil Creek approaching Little Bald Lookout, area are decent, but the higher you climb, the more challenging, rocky, and washed out the roads become. You might even end up sharing the road with a large band of domestic sheep and their stoic herder. A lot of visitors will probably turn back at or a bit before the Little Bald Spur. Before the spur, Road #1600 climbs past Saddle Camp. From here you may want to reassess the compatibility of your vehicle to the Clover Springs Road. From this point the #1600 becomes, practically, a 4x4 route mostly due to rutting.

(2) From Nile Flats

If you choose the Nile Flats route from the East you will turn off Highway 410 at the Wood Shed restaurant, and drive on the paved Nile Loop Road to Forest Road # 1600. Turn left and progress into

Nile flats, a large, open area several miles up where several roads branch off in different directions. Stay on Road #1600. From here you will wind around through the forest for approximately 12 miles, until you see a sign for the #1600-231 Little Bald Lookout Spur. Turn here to access the Lookout.

Coming from the west on Highway 410, turn off the upper entrance of the Nile Loop Road, one mile east of Sprick Park (Nile Valley Days event location). Watch for the #1600 Clover Springs Road to the right and you will be at Nile Flats in no time.

(3) From Halfway Flats

Halfway Flats is on the other side of the Naches River from Sawmill Campground and Highway 410. You access Halfway Flats by turning off Highway 410 one mile west of the Little Naches Road #1900. Cross the river and stay on Road #1709 until it meets up with Road #1706. Go back to the Cliffdell directions above and start at the junction of Roads #1709 and #1706, progressing on to the Little Bald Spur #1600-231

(4) Hiking or motorbike Trail #961 from Halfway Flats

If you are a glutton for punishment and want a long uphill hike, cross the #1709 Bridge and follow the road to the left down the river to the **Halfway Flats** camping area. Watch for Trail #961 on the right, park in a shady spot and let the suffering begin. Your ultimate destination is Saddle Camp, two miles past Little Bald Lookout on Road #1600. Some of this hike is a geologic wonderland.

This is an interesting though long trail with lots of views and some unique rock features. The best way to see it is from Saddle Camp, hiking back downhill.

NOTE: Schneider Springs fire: The 2021 Schneider Springs Fire was one of the largest uncontrolled local forest fires in memory, burning over 105,000 acres. It. started from a lightening bust along the Clover Springs Wilderness boundary and generally ran uncontrolled to the #1600 - #1709 road loop between the Nile Community and Halfway flats to the west. If you are interested in viewing the resulting devastation of this fire follows the route to Little Bald Lookout and view to the west of the Halfway Fats - Nile road loop.

TWO RETURN ROUTES THAT OFFER INTERESTING SIDE TRIPS

Dropping back to Highway 410 from either Little. Bald or Clover Springs: If you visited Clover Springs or Little Bald from Cliffdell, or the other gravel road routes listed above you may want to **Return by way of Mud Springs.** This is a treacherous 4x4 jeep route that has one redeeming feature for hikers and mountain bikers: It travels downhill on a 4x4 roadway along the top of cliffs overlooking the heart of the William O. Douglas Wilderness and the fabled Rattlesnake Northfork Creek. Review the "Mud Springs to Clover Springs" directions in the Clover Springs Lookout (#18) section in this book for more information on this interesting hike.

OR Return to State Route 410 by way of **Boulder Cave**. The route back toward Camp Roganunda (near Cliffdell) leads you to the Boulder Cave parking lot where you can see an old CCC campground shelter, still in good shape. Boulder Cave is a unique slab cave created by Devil Creek undercutting a basalt layer which has since broken off and slipped to one side, creating an unusual opening, once popular with Thompson Bats until it was rediscovered by curious sightseers.

SEE ALSO

- Clover Springs Lookout, #18
- Gossett, Gretta: Lindsay Camp p. 472
- Edgar Rock Lookout #3

6

Miners Ridge Lookout Site

6,072 Feet Elevation, 6,082 Feet on the old sign

T15N, R11E, Section 12 (or close to the East Section boundary)

West of Bumping Lake on Miner's Ridge

ACCESS AT A GLANCE:

Bumping Lake Road access off Highway 410 and

by way of 4x4 jeep Road #1809 past Bumping Lake toward Swamp Lake Trailhead.

- Lookout Style/Year: - Older style hip roof, two story: 1934 – 1972.

- Facilities Present: Old garage foundation.

- Nearby Lookout and Observation Sites: American Ridge Lookout site #17,

Twin Sisters Lakes from Deep Creek Trailhead, Wilderness Trail #980.

- Fire Lookout Panorama Photo date: 1934.

- Difficulty getting to the lookout site on a scale of 1 (easy) to 5 (difficult)**: 4**

- Once there, difficulty to find the actual lookout remains on a scale of 1 (easy) to 5 (difficult)**: 2**

Miners Ridge is situated at the west end of the Bumping River Basin. The old lookout site is approached from the paved Bumping River Road #1800 and onto a primitive 4x4 Road #1809 going by Granite Lake. The views from Miners Ridge are outstanding, particularly into the William O. Douglas Wilderness to the west.

The lookout was constructed in 1933 and/or 1934 (Gossett and USDA Records). The garage and storage buildings were placed in 1934 and the toilet was placed in 1937. Little is known about the actual station or when it and the outbuildings were removed. All that remains is the garage foundation and footing pillars. A short climb takes you to the actual peak. Looking to the west you are graced with a remarkable view into Redrock Creek and Cougar Lake area and on west over the Pacific Crest, hiding behind House Rock. To the east is Bumping Lake, bordered by American Ridge (on the left, North) and Nelson's Ridge (on the right, South). The little lake directly below the peak is Root Lake, named for Ruben Root, a well-known mining speculator and prospector who resided at Goose Prairie at the turn of the century when Tom Fife was the de-facto mayor of all things "Goose Prairie".

AND, don't' forget, the locals still spell it with no space between Goose and Prairie, so lets just go along with them here and avoid any hard feelings.

The old Miners Ridge panorama photo has an interesting detail; an antenna typical of AM radio antennas. I'd have to guess that the lookout had an AM radio up there (1943!) or used it for some sort of radio reception or as a clothesline. Transistor radios and compact batteries were yet to be invented but "crystal radios" were common. This Miners Ridge Lookout was occupied by a number of Yakima residents. Allen New was a lookout in the late 1930's, Dave Wright in 1938 and Betty Gallant during World War II. Douglas Jones, the 1942 lookout gave his life in the Battle of the Bulge and is fondly remembered by his high school chums of that time.

SETTING

Miner's Ridge is a well-named landmark. Fueled by rumors in the late 1800s of a possible railroad route through the Cascades at this point. Mining prospectors once scoured the surrounding ridges and streams for signs of unclaimed mineral wealth. Copper and zinc assays seemed to fuel the fire that burns in every miner's heart. Tom Fife was one of the first, and probably the most famous, of these local prospectors who homesteaded **Gooseprairie (sic)**, found interesting mineral deposits on Miners Ridge, and staked claims in this area by 1890. Though minerals are present in this area in interesting concentrations, the speculative aspect of this endeavor vanished when the cross-Cascade railroad route failed to transpire.

Eventually, **Ruben Root, Cap Simmons, John McAllister**, and others staked additional claims nearby. The old Clara Mine, Blue Bird, Crosetti, Keystone, Black Jack, Iron Door, and Copper City Mines are a few of those now abandoned mineral claims. Though the ridges in this area may have some promising mineral content, the cost of transporting the ore to a foundry made it essentially worthless as a profitable enterprise.

Near here, **Tommy Amato**, the Japanese camp cook, was killed when the Clara Mine's kitchen woodpile collapsed on him as he was collecting wood to cook the evening meal. Tommy's body was packed in a dog sled from the Clara Mine to the American River by **Ira Ford** for his return home to Japan. Tommy's passing reminds us of various nationalities which contributed workers to the early mining and settling efforts in the Naches Basin: Tom Fife was from Scotland, Hindoo John from India, Ruben Root was an immigrant from Minnesota, and Bacon Rind Dick was from a now forgotten chow line.

Looking south into the Bumping area (as it rises to Cowlitz Pass) you will recognize a setting similar to Snoqualmie Pass as it was in 1860. The upper Bumping and Cowlitz Pass were surveyed numerous times for a railroad route between 1880 and 1910, not without reason as the Bumping Drainage from the American River is a relatively ideal railroad grade. The problem was, once you reach the Cascade Crest the topography becomes harsh and unaccommodating. Also, rumors of coal deposits on the west side from Fish Lake helped fuel rumors of an impending Railroad through the area, but the coal claims were sparse and unsustainable.

GETTING THERE

- (1) FROM Bumping Lake, Forest Road #1800
- TO Forest Granite Lake 4x4 jeep Route #1809, often impassable.
- (2) OR, this apparent road route may be more suitable for hiking.

Estimated roundtrip time from Bumping Lake is 3-4 hours. From Bumping Lake this trip requires a high clearance vehicle with strong tires and some fortitude, yours and the vehicle's JUST TO GET TO THE LOOKOUT TURNOFF. Due to snow pack don't plan on this trip until mid-July. A two-wheel drive (2WD) pick-up or SUV is probably not going to make the entire trip without protest.

To get to Miner's Ridge, turn off State Route 410 on to Bumping Lake paved road #1800, west from Whistln' Jack Lodge or east from Chinook Pass. Stay on Bumping Lake Road through Goose Prairie (sic). As you drive by the Boy Scout's Camp Fife you will see Tom Fife's old cabin and his final resting place on your right.

At Bumping Lake Dam, four miles beyond Goose Prairie, make a short side trip over the impoundment road toward Bumping Lake Marina. From the middle of the dam look directly up the lake and you will see Miners Ridge, towering over the lake and westward surroundings. American Ridge is the long ridge to your right and Nelson Ridge is to the South.

From Bumping Lake, head west along gravel Forest Road #1800 toward the Deep Creek turnoff #1808. Stay on the main #1800 Road to the right, toward Fish Lake Trailhead at the road end. About one mile past Deep Creek turnoff the #1809 Road to the left toward Granite Lake and Miner's Ridge Lookout.

From here you will follow the Granite Lake Road #1809 to Miners Ridge. The Granite Lake Road is a steady climb over very rough terrain. From Granite Lake the road is even more challenging. After several switchbacks you arrive at the 6,072 foot Miners Ridge peak. On a clear day the panoramic view is stunning.

As you return by Granite Lake stop at the second switchback as it sweeps to the left. From this point you may find a faint hiking trail around the hillside to the south into the old, abandoned **Clara Mine** area. Old dilapidated cabins there remain for your curiosity.

Hiking side trips on this route west of Bumping Lake include Fish Lake Trailhead, Swamp Lake Trailhead, and Twin Sister's Lake (or Deep Creek) Trailhead. The Swamp Lake Trail accesses the upper Bumping River Waterfalls. Fish Lake Trailhead accesses the Bumping River Trail to Fish Lake near the Pacific Crest Trail, and the Twin Sisters Lake Trailhead offers dispersed camping spurs and access to Twin Sisters Lakes and **Tumac Mt. Lookout, #20,** if you don't mind the long and tortuous drive. The Deep Creek Horse Camp, one mile before Twin Sisters Trailhead offers a good place for horseback riders to depart into the legislated Wilderness. As you explore up Road #1808 you will pass by Copper City turnoff, a short distance off the main road on a primitive spur road. It may be best to park along the main road and venture along the **Copper City** Access Road on foot.

SEE ALSO

- Nelson, Jack: *We Never Got Away*, a must read for local lore.
- - Gretta Gossett for history and incomparable background.
- - Tumac Mountain Lookout #20, this book
- - Metzkers 1934 map binder for section 12 line mapping
- - Cyr, Suzy, Tanum, the Story of Bumping Lake, 2022

7

Raven Roost Lookout Site

6,198 Feet Elevation - Present site somewhat lower

T18N, R12E, Section 22

Between Crow Creek and the Little Naches River
near the Cascade Crest

- ACCESS AT A GLANCE:

Highway 410 to paved Little Naches Forest Road #1900 and
onto Forest Road #1902
at Crow Creek Campground and then on 13 miles. Expect
wind on the Roost.
- **Lookout Style/Year:** - Older hip style roof without tower
1934 – 1965 (when the site was altered).
- **Facilities Present:** Site destroyed 1965, no historical facilities.
Faint evidence
of an old garage, south side of parking lot, outstanding view
and landmark radio facility towers are recognizable for
miles around.
- **Nearby Lookout and Observation Sites**: Arch Rock Trail Shelter
#22 this book
and the eyeball-to-eyeball view of Fife Peak to the South
and Mt. Rainier to the West.
- **Fire Lookout Panorama Photo date**: 1934.
- **Difficulty getting to the lookout site** on a scale of 1 (easy) to 5
(difficult): **2**
- **Once there, difficulty to find the actual lookout remains** on a
scale of 1 (easy) to 5 (difficult): **1**

R aven Roost is a promontory overlooking much of the Little Naches Basin, Manastash Ridge and the north side of Fife Peak, which
is a natural monument to the memory of Tom Fife. The Roost is one
of the unique road accessed viewpoints in the Little Naches, in part
because of the relatively good road and the great view of Mt. Rainier. If
you look closely into the Little Naches Drainage to the North you may
be able to trace the general route of the Longmire Wagon Train as the
pioneers crossed Naches Pass north of here in 1853. The Raven Roost
site is now occupied by several microwave tower facilities in the early
stages of abandonment resulting from advances in technology.

The "Raven Roost" name was probably an association with the
adjacent "Crow Creek", back in the time when there wasn't that
much difference between ravens and crows. This lookout was
constructed in 1934 to cover the northern portion of the Naches
Ranger District which at that time hosted a large number of sheep
bands. (a sheep band is around 1,000 sheep but can be stretched to
2,000, Ewes and lambs) The early station was serviced from Crow
Creek Guard Station (long since gone) near the mouth of Crow
Creek and to the left and above the bridge you crossed 13 miles ago.

Electricity was brought in underground to Raven Roost in 1964 but it
took another year to finish the flattening of the top and the instillation
of microwave tower facilities. The entire peak was altered but you
may find evidence of a garage foundation if you search the south
edge of the existing parking lot. Raven Roost can be accessed by
passenger car up to the final 1/4 mile: The challenging road up to
the final ¼ mile is a small price to pay for such a outstanding view.

Local lookouts at Raven Roost include Dick Simmons of Naches
who was the last lookout of record in 1965. Dick began working on
the District trail crew at age 16 and eventually retired from the Forest
Service sometime after it was consolidated with the Tieton District,
around 1982. A historical photo of Raven Roost from around
1936 indicates that Ralph Cramer was also a lookout at The Roost,
back in the day when lookouts were called "Rangers".

SETTING

In 1936 a Civilian Conservation Corps (CCC) crew constructed the road to Raven Roost and on to Cougar Valley. Their side camp was at Huckleberry Camp, two miles east of and below the Roost where they found a good water and suitable camping. When the crew departed in the fall they assumed they would return in the spring to extend the Cougar Valley Road deeper into Crow Creek. However, when spring came, other priorities had developed and the Cougar Valley Trailhead simply became the end of the line. The old photo panorama from Raven Roost shows the Cougar Valley Trail, generally where the eventual road was constructed by the CCC crew. It can be surmised the road construction crew simply crawled down the ridge on the general location of the old Cougar Valley Trail.

Later, in an effort to make the trailhead more useful to horsemen and to avoid a large sidehill cut at Cougar Valley, the Forest Service reluctantly closed the road near the top of Raven Roost where the trailhead remains today. The trail to **Cougar Valley** is now a testament to the fact that roads make good trails, a reverse of the "trail to road" Forest Service timber program of the 1960s and 70s. The trail to Cougar Valley is mostly outside Wilderness but from Cougar Valley both trails (One accessing the Pacific Crest Trail) are all within Norse Peak Wilderness and limited to foot travel. A day hike down to Cougar Valley and back is an easy saunter through open hillsides with outstanding views. The Norse Peak Fire of 2017 burned over this trail and you'll look a while before finding such a perfect illustration of Wilderness fire mosaic patterns so graphically close at hand and so easy to observe.

GETTING THERE

- FROM Highway 410, turn onto the paved Little Naches Road #1900.
- FOLLOWING FS Road #1900 for several miles

to the #1902 Road and on 13 miles, turning right at the short Spur #866

to stay on the main road and on to the top of the ridge and lookout site,

OR visit the Cougar Valley trailhead at the end of spur Road #1902-866.

Estimated trip time from the mouth of Little Naches River is 3-5 hours. Drive west from Yakima on Highway 12 to the junction with Highway 410. Follow SR 410 thirty or so miles west and turn off onto paved Little Naches Forest Road # 1900 a couple of miles west of Whistln' Jack Lodge.

Several miles up the #1900 Road you will pass Kaner Flat Campground. Directly after the campground turn west (left) on Forest Road #1902 and cross the Little Naches River. In a mile or so the road will make a right turn across Crow Creek at Crow Creek Campground, near the site of the old Crow Creek Guard Station on the left. Stay on Road #1902 for 13 miles to the Raven Roost Trailhead turnoff. Turn right onto the main road and proceed up the hill to the top of Raven Roost. Here a huge parking lot and steady wind will greet you. The left trailhead spur, a short distance to the ridge, offers suitable camping, and an unforgettable view of Mt. Rainier on a clear day.

Raven Roost Road is usually suitable for SUV and two-wheel drive pickups but without four wheel drive, the final ¼ mile may require a hike. Don't forget, in these conditions YOU can do some necessary road work by tossing boulders to the side and planning a "line" or route up through the rough spots. If you accompany jeeps in the Forest you will quickly realize that the greatest advantage they have isn't their extra two drive wheels, but their experience in identifying and executing a "line" up through a rough spot, which brings up my theory of negotiating rough forest roads: The most important equipment in getting back is probably strong tires and a two wheel vehicle with extra strong tires can go a long ways on some mighty bad roads. After tires, clearance is the second most important piece of equipment to help you get there. Driving ability is of course a big factor in "getting home, but don't forget, almost as many people have gotten stuck **because** of their four wheels as have gotten unstuck (technically, the numbers are exactly equal). The Forest Service rule for 4x4 use was once, "Drive until you get stuck, throw it in 4x4 to get unstock and then head for home". In this case, the guy who gets home is the one who recognizes the point where it was wiser to get out and walk and let his vehicle rest a bit.

There is an unspoken phenomena related to lookout access roads. While they generally deteriorate the further you go, the final /1/4 mile is often more difficult out of scale with the lower sections. Why this is remains a mystery, but perhaps it was to discourage visitors, or to discourage fickle lookouts. Quartz Mountain, Red Top in the Swauk, Timberwolf, Raven Roost, and many other lookouts display this tendency to make the final ¼ mile of a lookout visit a memorable one.

Hiking access to the Pacific Crest Trail from Raven Roost Trailhead is unique as this is the only real east side road access point between Chinook Pass and Pyramid Peak.

Note: The maps do NOT call this "Raven's Roost". Guess there must have been only one Raven.

SEE ALSO
- Spring, Ira: Raven Roost Lookout site (and microwave towers) is featured in *Lookouts*, p. 161.

8

Timberwolf Mountain
Lookout Site

6,391 feet elevation

T15N, R13E, Section 25

Between Highways 12 and 410 near Bethel Ridge

- ACCESS AT A GLANCE:

Forest Road #1500 from two points off either Highway 12 or
Highway 410, and on
to Spur #190, turning west to the lookout and passing the old
stable at Timberwolf Meadows.
- **Lookout Style/Year:** - Older style, 1931 – 1972 (may be as late
as 1975).
- **Facilities Present:** Standard horse barn in nearby pasture, generic
modern outhouse.
- **Nearby Lookout and Observation Sites:** (1) Bethel Ridge
Overlook, see below
(2) Cash Prairie views, turn west on Spur #1500-199 (3)
Rattlesnake Spring
(an old camping area near the junction of Roads #1500 and
#1502)
and the MJB Trailhead some ways south of the Timberwolf
spur on Road #1500.
- **Fire Lookout Panorama Photo date**: 1934.
- **Difficulty getting to the lookout site** on a scale of 1 (easy) to 5
(difficult): **3**

- Once there, difficulty to find the actual lookout remains on a scale of 1 (easy) to 5 (difficult)**: 2**

Timberwolf Mountain Lookout site is located at the top of Timberwolf Mountain, north of Bethel Ridge, centered within the Rattlesnake Creek drainage. Though the rounded peak made an ideal ground level lookout, it is not a dominant geographic feature. Views from Timberwolf include Cleman Mountain to the east, Mt. Rainier to the west, Manastash Ridge and Rattlesnake Peak to the north, and a short southern view to Bethel Ridge, which is a few feet higher. The commanding view is into and up Rattlesnake Creek Basin to the west.

Timberwolf Lookout Station was originally constructed in 1931 at a cost of $562.79 and survived until 1975. The lookout was of the older design, with a gable roof, called an "L-4 style lookout building" by Kresek. Older style lookouts were smaller, with smaller individual glass window panes, a product of the times, as are we all. The roof was a peaked "hip" style with no eves and a single shutter on each side, hinged from the top. The shutters were dropped in the winter for protection from snow, which in conjunction with wind and a few broken glass panes, is a lookout killer. The building was constructed on a small rocky platform.

The Timberwolf Lookout was removed by Youth Conservation Corp (YCC) crews in the mid 1970's and burned at a different location. That station was unique because it had a small cellar beneath the floor to provide cool storage for the lookout's provisions, an unusual feature appreciated by the Timberwolf lookouts. Mildred McMurray, with her husband Harry, resided here for 10 summers between 1950 and 1964 remembered packing the cellar with snow from the nearby snowbank, providing an efficient refrigerator in the early fire season.

It was common for lookouts, particularly those at high elevation, to prize their late melting snow banks for food storage and cold drinks. A snow bank was the only way a lookout could enjoy the most prized of all lookout food groups: Jello! However, remember these lookouts were at mountain peak elevations and relatively cool when compared to summer temps in Yakima. For example, Jumpoff summer day time temps seldom exceeded 79F.

The garage and barn were both placed in 1934. The Timberwolf Barn was a unique structure that survived until recently when it was destroyed by the Schneider Springs fire of 2021. Its' foundation is there to find in a lower meadow. Technically called a "Fireman's Stable" this old barn was an outstanding example of a historic structure associated with old lookouts, particularly if they were required to keep a horse. The garage which once stood at the base of this site, 80 yards to the south, is no longer standing. The unique original outhouse stands to the north of the site in disrepair but serviceable to those inclined. Bring your own TP.

Ron Kobelin of Roseburg Oregon was stationed at Timberwolf in 1942 – 44 and Leo Simmons of Yakima was there in 1946, possibly 1947. Harry McMurray and his wife Mildred spent 10 years looking for smokes there (1950 – 64). Jim and Sandy Kohl served on Timberwolf in 1964 (their honeymoon) and Gary Freelan from California was the last watcher to occupy this station.

SETTING

Take binoculars on this trip and scan the surrounding peaks and talus slopes for white dots, known locally as mountain goats. This goat herd graces Timberwolf Mountain probably because several fires along this ridge over the past 50 years have improved their habitat. Somehow Timberwolf Lookout survived those flames. Pay particular attention to **Meeks Table**, a unique basalt table Research Natural Area to the North, named for a former lookout guard at Mt. Aix Lookout #19. If you encounter goats remember this is their home: Respect their privacy and do not attempt to save them or their young from their wild natural environment. It has been said that Rattlesnake Creek was named for its twisty path and is not home to Rattlesnakes. The Rattlesnakes you encounter at Meek's Table will not argue.

Sheepherders once knew this area well. Cash Prairie was named for "Short and Dirty" Cash (See "Blue Slide Lookout #1). The MJB trailhead deserves a description below in the "Other Good Views" section, a few paragraphs below. Carpenter Springs, just to the south of Bethel Ridge near the #1500 road was another favorite stop for packers during the sheep era.

GETTING THERE

- (1) FROM the Woodshed Restaurant, Highway SR 410: Road #1500 to Spur #190.

- (2) OR FROM Hause Creek on Highway 12, Road #1500 to the 190 Spur, 9 miles.

- Some may choose to walk the last ¼ mile.

Though remote, Timberwolf can be visited throughout the summer in a sedan, SUV, or truck with good tires though you should expect the unexpected and abide by the rules of backcountry visits. At 6,391 feet in elevation, it is higher than most of the nearby Wilderness area and offers views to rival those on more remote peaks. A snow bank here lingers later into the summer than surrounding areas. Don't get stuck. The south slopes of Rattlesnake Creek to the north of Timberwolf Mountain are ideal winter mountain goat habitat. Like Rattlesnakes they are not to be bothered.

Plan ahead, fill your gas tank before leaving town, take the 10 essentials, and don't ask your vehicle to do something that it is incapable of delivering.

You will need to start at the North or South entrance to the Bethel Ridge Road #1500. The south end connects to U.S. Highway 12 a short distance west of Hause Creek Campground. The north entrance connects to State Route 410 at Eagle Rock (Woodshed Restaurant). This loop trip between highways is a remarkable drive, with many unique views. Plan a full day and make the entire Bethel Ridge circuit if time permits.

Approximately 1/2 the way (either direction) you will see the Timberwolf Spur #190. Turn west. Progress along this road approximately 2 1/2 miles to the peak. You may see the foundation of the old horse barn in one of the lower meadows. Please show respect for this old relic and leave it as you find it. It has endured many a harsh winter and deserves an extended retirement.

Timberwolf Lookout is a good place to initiate a discussion about maps, signing, and phantoms. Not to pick on the Forest Service maps, or signing practices, or even phantom locations but you are safest to start your trip by reviewing your map. Remember, signs fall off or are stolen and they are often designed by someone in an office and placed by someone who is lost. Roads can be closed from a variety of influences, road numbers float like a log in a lake, or sink, and map makers often get just as confused as their abstraction of reality may not depend on knowing something concrete about the land. Anyone visiting the forest needs to glance at their map from time to avoid confusion, It's called, "map reading". Always follow the hiking guideline for getting found: If the road is going downhill, it's probably going home, uphill heads for heaven.

OTHER GOOD VIEWS

(1) Bethel Ridge Overlook: As a regular Forest Service field worker with compass training I was often sent to a high point with a truck and a compass during lightning storms. One spot I have spent many a sleepless night in a cramped pickup was the Bethel Ridge overlook just under and south of the Bethel Ridge Microwave tower, with views into the Tieton Basin that were not available to the nearby Timberwolf Lookout. You can visit that remarkable view off the Bethel Ridge road by way of the #1500-324 Spur.

(2) OR you can also visit **Cash Prairie**, three miles south of the lookout and west of the #1500 Road on the #1500-199 Spur. The view from the trailhead is unique and Cash Prairie Trailhead also offers outstanding hiking to the west on the ridge top Burnt Mountain Trail #1141 as it wanders toward the head of the Rattlesnake Creek by way of Burnt Mt., Shellrock Peak, Russell Ridge, Ironstone Mountain, and McNeil Peak, all accessible from this ridge trail.

(3) Five miles west of Eagle Rock the old Hanging Tree area reminds us that portions of the Gary Cooper movie of that name were filmed near here. A cabin scene from that movie was filmed at the long forgotten **Rattlesnake Springs Guard Station** near the junction of the #1500 and # 1502 Roads. The actual "Hanging Tree" was rumored to be further down the #1500 Road, but fact or fiction it is now just a memory.

(4) MJB Trailhead: Four miles south of Timberwolf Lookout is a unique trailhead with an interesting history. MJB was once marked with a coffee can on a post, directing the sheep band packer the way to the herder. The old, actual, trailhead is 100 yards south of the more hospitable existing trailhead. A short stroll south of the present trailhead is a small but scenic basalt hoodo dyke rock feature poking up as if asking to be photographed. The MJB Trail is a long, 48 switchback drop to the creek below. The upper portion of this trail is scenic and inviting on the downward portion but you will be so thankful to have the switchbacks behind you on the return trip that you will hardly notice.

SEE ALSO

- **McMurray:** *Lookout Story*, elsewhere in this book
- MJB Trailhead (Trail #1101, two miles south of the Lookout turnoff

> on #1500 Road offers a splendid trail down to Rattlesnake Creek
>
> to the campsite logically known as "KOA" by Wilderness Rangers.

- Timberwolf Mountain, Gossett, *Beyond the Bend*: p. 487
- Hiler, Mike: *The Head of the Snake,* Pack And Paddle

Non-Wilderness Sites Managed with Adjacent Districts

There are a number of old lookout sites located on the boundary ridge tops defining Yakima County and/or the Wenatchee National Forest. Some of those lookouts were managed by the Naches District, some were managed by the neighboring district, and a few were jointly managed. Because some of those lookouts are only a few feet from the county line, or located on the line, or more likely no one has any idea the exact county of those lookout buildings, and because they look down into the Naches Basin, I have included them to this guide for completeness.

There is generally a road or something that resembles a road to these sites

But motorized access may be challenging

Plan ahead, carry the 10 essentials, travel safely!

GOAT PEAK
LOOKOUT
AMERICAN RIDGE
SNOQUALMIENE
ELEV
473

E. BROWN

9

(Big) Bald Mountain Lookout Site

5,898 Feet Elevation, the old sign indicated 5,906 feet elevation

Elevation estimates vary as much as 175 feet

T17N, R15E, Section 15

Kittitas County, Manastash Ridge and Cleman Mountain

Lookout was USFS constructed and managed on private timber land

- ACCESS AT A GLANCE:

Off Highway 410, east of Whistlin' Jack Lodge taking Forest Service Bald Mountain Road #1701
and traveling 12 miles over roads that may be challenging to a short hike. Or a rewarding hike
from the end of Gold Creek Road #1703 (often closed) by way of Spring Creek Road #1705

- Lookout Style/Year: - Small day-use cabin and tower 1934 – 1955, tower 1932 – 1955?

- A tower was completed in 1955, variety of facilities removed 1972.

- Facilities Present: Evidence of foundation and guy wires.

- Nearby Observation Sites: Cleman Mountain. Lookout #10, Devil's Slide Overlook #2,

Canteen Flats, Quartz Mountain Lookout #18 (Cle Elum Ranger District).

- Fire Lookout Panorama Photo Date: 1929 and 1934.

- Difficulty getting to the lookout site on a scale of 1 (easy) to 5 (difficult): **3**

- Once there, difficulty to find the actual lookout remains on a scale of 1 (easy) to 5 (difficult): **2**

Bald Mountain or "Big Bald" (as it is known, to separate it from "Little" Bald Lookout #5) is located at a promontory along Manastash Ridge, north of Cleman Mountain. Big Bald is accessible both from the Wenas Basin (4x4 high clearance vehicle required) and from Highway 410 along the gravel Bald Mountain Forest Road #1701. Either trip offers great views of Manastash and Umptanum Ridges, Devil's Creek, the upper Wenas Basin, and the lower reaches of the Little Naches Basin.

The Bald Mountain Lookout panorama photo from 1934 shows a small cabin to the east of the tower. Packy Howatt was stationed here in 1931 and made some of the early improvements. He remembered finding stray bummer lambs, lost from the large bands of sheep which were ranged there, and which he would occasionally invite in for dinner.

The first lookout tower at this location was erected after 1931and a lookout summer residence was placed in 1934. A newer tower was installed in 1955 along with storage shed, toilet and garage. Those later foundations are still visible. Bald Mountain was abandoned in 1972 and the lookout building sold to Bud Fisk, a local former lookout and private timber manager (see Blue Slide Lookout #1). The Bald Mountain peak and the old lookout site are presently on private logging land but access is not restricted. Although it may seem strange that a Forest Service station was once placed on private land, you must remember that before bureaucracy the forest was a neighborly place of share and share alike.

The old Quartz Mt. Lookout #14 was located about 10 miles further to the northwest along this ridge. That site can be visited in a high clearance vehicle over forest roads from the town of Tharp by way of the Taneum Forest Road #33 system, or from Bald Mountain by motorbike, mountain bike, horseback, or by hiking. The 1" per mile "Fireman's Map" of the Cle Elum District will assist you when traveling in that area.

A Civilian Conservation Corps worker, George Jones, was stationed at Bald Mountain around 1943 (he was 17 years old). Some records indicate that a William J. "Firehouse Bill" Jones may have served time there as well as packing ponies at one time for the Naches District. But Packy Howett, the first lookout there, "owns" the distinction as "THE Bald Mountain Lookout".

SETTING

The Sprick Park/Elk Ridge area, near the mouth of Benton Creek (not to be mistaken with Barton Creek near Bumping Lake), is a unique historical place in Washington history. Near here, in 1853 the Longmire Wagon Train descended to the Naches River from the Wenas Basin by way of Rocky Prairie. Fifty-three wagons, headed for Puget Sound in late October, were racing the weather as their group passed near this point. From here the wagons progressed up the Naches River, on into the Little Naches Basin, and over the Cascade Crest near **Naches Pass**. They camped at Government Meadows (See Pyramid Peak, Lookout #13) a few days and then descended into the Greenwater drainage on their way to Steilacoom.

As you drive up the Bald Mountain #1701 Road your open view up the ridge highlights the courage and tenacity of those pioneers, and the oxen who pulled the 53 wagons. At this site portions of the Audie Murphy Movie "To Hell and Back" were filmed in the early 1950s. Sprick Park, almost directly across Highway 410 from the entry to the Bald Mountain Road may be a good place to RV camp if the Sprick Park folks are not hosting an event or fair.

Rocky Prairie, the point where Road #1701 breaks out on the ridge, was probably a resting spot of the Longmire Wagon Train. Lela Linker, Longmire descendent, remembers this spot as a one day grazing stop when she assisted her father driving cattle between the Wenas Basin and the Naches Basin in the 1920s and 30s. Rocky Prairie, which hosts some aspen groves, was likely a Native American campsite where early residents harvested roots along this ridge. Members of the Wilkes Pacific Exploring Expedition (1841) as well as **George Brinton McClellan, John Edgar, Theodore Winthrop, Andy Burge, Chief Kamiakin** and other pioneers and explorers likely visited this general area when crossing the Cascades in the 1850s.

When you reach Bald Mountain you are on private logging company lands. Show the same respect for these lands as you would for your National Forest. Your efforts will help keep these areas open for public use and show appreciation to the private landowners for your visit.

GETTING THERE

- (1) FROM Highway 410 near Sprick Park over FS Road #1701

TO Forest Road spur #530 (around 12 miles) to the north.

Park at the end of Spur #530 and hike

a short way uphill to the lookout site,

(2) OR FROM Highway 410 over the Rock Creek Forest Road #1702 which ties in to

the Bald Mountain Road #1701 near Canteen Flats and then on to Bald Mountain.

(3) OR **Devil's Slide:** Flip back to the Devil's Slide Overlook, #2 this book

for yet another Bald Mountain Lookout side trip.

Plan a full day for this drive by adding hiking and exploring on the return route. On a clear day the view west from Bald Mt is stunning.

Several side trips offer outstanding views and unique opportunities for viewing wildlife and spring foliage. If you have time and the right vehicle, or don't mind the 13 mile round trip, don't miss the side trip to Cleman Mt Lookout #10 from Rocky Prairie. The core of this trip from Highway 410 is suitable for the family sedan or SUV but side trips and early and late season visits require high clearance vehicles with strong tires.

SIDE TRIPS

(1) The spring wild flowers at Rocky Prairie and Canteen Flats are at their peak in early to mid May (most years) and offer amazing views and great photography. The gravel road has some challenging "slow" spots and a 4x4 is generally required for the last ½ mile to the lookout particularly in the early spring and late fall. If you encounter snow banks blocking the road, do not challenge them as the road bed is very soft at the snow bank melting edges and you risk "sinking into" the muddy road.

(2) The Rock Creek, Rocky Prairie Loop: This trip offers unique forest edge and transition forest zone topography in the Bald Mountain area between Cleman Lookout and Manastash Ridge. Proceed off Highway 410 up Rock Creek Road # 1702. At Canteen Flats, Road #1701, turns north toward Bald Mt. or south and return to Highway 410 through Rocky Prairie. From Rocky Prairie Road junctions you can continue along the ridge south to Cleman Lookout (site # 10 this book) or return to Highway 410 on the Bald Mt. Road # 1701. A Forest Service map is advised for this trip as many interesting non-system (un-numbered) jeep routes present themselves throughout this route, for your confusion. Open area hiking on this ridge is at its best early summer through October when it slowly turns into a snowmobile and X-Country ski adventure.

(3) Both **Cleman Mt. Lookout #10 and Devil's Slide Overlook** #2 can be visited the same day you visit Bald Mountain. See those instructions in other sections of this book. A Forest Service map is advised for these trips as many interesting non-system jeep routes present themselves throughout this route. Open country hiking is easy along this ridge top. Motor vehicle travelers are encouraged to avoid vegetation damage by staying on the system roads.

SEE ALSO:

- Cleman Mountain Lookout #10 this book for more directions and history

- Quartz Mountain Lookout #14

- See my sketch to Packy Howatt in "*Buckskin Larch and Bedrock*", p.38

10

Cleman Mountain Lookout Site

5,062 Feet Elevation

T15N, R16E, Section 5

UTM Grid: N46-49.416, W128-51.30

Washington State Game land north and west of Naches, WA

- ACCESS AT A GLANCE:

Highway 410 east of Whistlin' Jack Lodge 5 miles, turning east on the Bald Mt. Road #1701
to Rocky Prairie and on 6 miles south to the lookout over a 4x4 jeep road.
- **Lookout Style and Year: -** Older Log Cabin 1946 - 1954,
- Newer lookout with 40' tower, 1968,
- Emergency use into the 1970s (Kresek).
- **Facilities Present:** tower footings, land shapes, and modern electronic equipment.
- **Nearby Lookout and Observation Sites:** (Big) Bald Mt Lookout #9.
- **No known Fire Lookout Panorama Photo** as this was a DNR / WDFW facility.
- **Difficulty getting to the lookout site** on a scale of 1 (easy) to 5 (difficult): **4**
- **Once there, difficulty to find the actual lookout remains** on a scale of 1 (easy) to 5 (difficult): **3**

Cleman Mountain is the monolithic stone north and west of the town of Naches. Named for local pioneer Augustan Cleman

75

the father of John Cleman, the lookout was originally constructed on the Peak of Cleman Mountain around 1954 and rebuilt on a 40 Foot tower in 1968. A huge landslide on the west side of Cleman Mountain, known as the "Sanford Pasture Slide" occurred before settlement. The west side of Cleman Mountain is relatively unstable with local slides extending into the Naches River as recently as 2013.

This lookout was a State Fish and Wildlife Department managed tower shared with the Forest Service during the late 1980s. The station and tower eventually suffered disrepair and subsequently blew over around 2007. This lookout viewed into the lower Naches Basin and up into Oak Creek, the Nile Basin and parts of the lower Naches Basin. The Tieton Basin was hidden from Cleman's view but the Cleman Station could triangulate on Jumpoff Lookout #4 and Jumpoff Lookout could easily spot Cleman to the east, perfect for aligning their map and calibrating the firefinder compass.

The old station was removed by Bud Fisk, and is presently the sun room at the old McCafferty's Saw Shop (now a residence) in the upper Nile community along Highway 410, though some claim that sunroom migrated from Bald Mountain, which seems more likely. Modern electronic facilities remain scattered about. Lee Scott, son-in-law of Boone Richey, served on Cleman Lookout in 1953.

SETTING

John Cleman and his brother, sons of Augustan Cleman walked the first band of sheep into the Yakima Basin for their father, who was homesteading near Naches. Cleman Mountain was originally named Burge Mountain honoring Andy J. Burge, but the name was later changed to Cleman Mountain owing to the importance of the Cleman family as local pioneers.

GETTING THERE

For instructions to visit Cleman Mountain, read the *Getting There* instructions for Bald Mt. Lookout #9. Also, see the Forest Service *Roaded Trips Guide* handout available at the Naches Station.

FROM Sprick Park (Elk Ridge, Nile Valley Days location), 6 mile
east of Whistln' Jack Lodge on
Highway 410 TO Rocky Prairie on the Bald Mountain
Road #1701 four miles,
THEN 6 miles south over the Cleman Mountain 4x4 jeep
Road #1712.

To begin your trip, drive west from Naches on Highway 410 to Sprick Park (Nile Valley Days, Elk Ridge). From here the gravel Bald Mountain Road #1701 climbs to the east through Rocky Prairie, Canteen Flats, and on to Big Bald Mountain. Turning south at Rocky Prairie you can follow the 4x4 jeep Road #1712, (not to be mistaken for spur Road #1713) 6 miles to the top of Cleman Mt. and the site of the old Cleman Lookout.

The Cleman Mt. Lookout Road #1712 is a rewarding hike but is challenging on a hot summer day as there is little shade while the 'ups and downs" add to the overall exertion. If you travel with any mode of transportation be sure to take extra water. There are numerous other routes to the lookout from the North Wenas Road you may consider. Water Works Canyon Trail, near the highway 410 - 12 junction is a good option for hikers. Don't try these routes unless you have a map and know how to use it. Please respect locked gates and private roads.

SEE ALSO

- Bald Mountain Lookout 39

- Devils Slide Lookout, #2 this book

- Gossett, Gretta: *Beyond the Bend*, Ye Galleon Press, 1979 for many nearby references

11

Darland Mountain Lookout Site

6,981 feet elevation

T12N, R13E, Section 20

Divide Ridge South of Conrad Meadow

Jointly managed: Forest Service and State Department of Natural Resources

- **ACCESS AT A GLANCE:** 4X4 jeep trail off Forest Service and State DNR roads
    from Ahtanum Basin Road systems west of Wiley City.
- **Lookout Style/Year:** - Older cupola cabin 1925 – 1936, more modern cabin 1936 – 1966.
- **Facilities Present:** Some evidence of concrete lookout foundations, cables, and modern radio
    relay equipment managed by Yakima Sheriff's office.
- **Nearby Lookout and Observation Points:** Blue Slide Lookout site #1
    Access to the Divide Ridge Trail.
- **No known Fire Lookout Panorama Photo** for this site.
- **Difficulty getting to the lookout site** on a scale of 1 (easy) to 5 (difficult): **4**
- **Once there, difficulty to find the actual lookout remains** on a scale of 1 (easy) to 5 (difficult): **2**

Located on Darland Mountain, just inside the National Forest Boundary along Divide Ridge, Darland Mountain Lookout is often mentioned but seldom visited. The remarkable view from this point looks into Goat Rocks Wilderness, the Tieton South Fork Basin and Conrad Meadows, and on over to Bear Creek Mountain, and even down the Tieton Basin a bit. "Darlin" must have been named for an early sheep herder as this was prime sheep grazing country from the time when Scottish sheep herders were just discovering this area and when local names were becoming local landmarks. Before the Forest Service was designated an early ranger station was located in the upper Ahtanum where the sheep bands entered the almost virgin upper country. Later, after the Forest Service was formed, the ranger station moved down into the Tieton Basin near what is now Bear Cove at a spot aptly named **"White Horse"** for the white horses the early ranger rode when monitoring sheep bands.

SETTING

"Darling" Mountain is known from the tales of **William O. Douglas** in his famous local history and boyhood memory *Of Men and Mountains*. Douglas called it Darling or "Darlin" Mountain for some reason that has never been explained, and his visits there preceded the lookout tower by a decade or two.

The Bill Douglas stories of those days, around 1917, are revealing of the times when Yakima youth would hike out their front doors with nothing but a horseshoe backpack (a rolled blanket, lashed with a rope and filled with a few basic food items) slung over their shoulders. In one adventure Douglas worked his way west onto Divide Ridge and then glissaded the early spring snow slopes of "Darling Mountain" on a cast iron cook pan, or so the story goes.

GETTING THERE

FROM Yakima City through Tampico by the Ahtanum Road:

Drive west from Yakima on the Ahtanum Road system, progressing through Wiley City. At Tampico the road splits at the old Tampico

Store site. Head on the northwest branch past the Ahtanum Guard station. From this point drive west a dozen miles to the top of Darland Mt. on the Ahtanum North Fork road system. You will encounter, and have to make decision about, a number of unmarked roads so carry a good map, preferably the Naches Ranger Station 1 inch to the mile *Fireman's Map*.

Hiking: Darland lookout can of course be accessed on foot over the Divide Ridge Trail. Coming from the east (Louie Gap Way, see directions to Jumpoff Lookout #4) or from the west by way of Klickitat Meadows accessed from Conrad Meadows in the Tieton South Fork. Parts of this route are also known as the Gray Rock 4x4 trail and Klickton Divide. However, if you are up to the adventure of these general routes you don't need my two cents worth here. Consider this trip an exploratory adventure; I've been there several times and each time new challenges awaited. The trail along Divide Ridge breaches Dome Peak, passes through Narrow Neck Gap, and offers outstanding views the whole way to the south and down into the Tieton Basin at Louey Gap Way.

SEE ALSO

- Douglas, William O.: *Of Men and Mountains*, Chapter 4

- Blue Slide Lookout, # 1

12

Pine Mountain Lookout Site

4,300 - 4,301 Feet Elevation

T13N, R15E, Section 25

Washington State Department of Natural Resources managed

Private Ownership, overlooking Tampico to the East

- ACCESS AT A GLANCE:

Near Tampico, west of Yakima on the paved Ahtanum Road, turning north on the North Fork Ahtanum Road and on by way of Nasty Creek Road.

Please, NO access without landowner permission.

- Lookout Style and Year: 14'X14, flat Roof, 35 foot tower.

First Lookout building: 1961, removed sometime between 2006 and 2012.

- Facilities Present: None, private land, gated.

- No Panorama Photograph, State Lookout

- Difficulty getting to the lookout site on a scale of 1 (easy) to 5 (difficult): **5**

- Once there, difficulty to find the actual lookout remains on a scale of 1 (easy) to 5 (difficult): **3**

Pine Mountain Lookout was located on the ridge directly west of Tampico. The drainage to the south flows into the Yakima River near Union Gap while the drainage to the north flows into Naches

River near Selah Gap. There is no significant view from Pine Mountain into the Tieton Basin or further north.

Wendy Warren and her relief, Debbie Mortimer served at Pine Mt 1978-79. Wendy also served at Gray Back Lookout in Kittitas County in 1974. Wendy is a local Yakima artist and writer, and her firsthand story of working on a lookout is included in this book. Thanks Wendy!

SETTING

Some of the first settlers in the Yakima Basin chose transition forest edges where pine and oak forests meet and where streams are more accessible for farming. This mix of open grazing, building timber, and available water for irrigation supplied a mix of resources necessary for the early homesteaders. Here Garry Oak and ponderosa pine, along with elderberry and sagebrush characterize the edges of the fir forest stretching onto and over the Cascade Crest. **A. J. Splawn,** one of the early settlers and the first mayor of Yakima chose such a site along Cowiche Creek for his ranch. Anyone who has visited the Ahtanum Mission will get an idea of the lower elevation geographical setting around Pine Mountain Lookout.

GETTING THERE

From Tampico drive northwest on the Ahtanum North Fork Road to Nasty Creek Road and on to the lookout on the Pine Mt. Road. Public access ends at the locked gate defining private land. The old Pine Mt. lookout site is located on private land, and I don't recommend visiting this site unless you have specific approval from the landowner. Pine Mountain can be seen from many locations along Divide and Jumpoff Ridges and from Ahtanum Ridge to the South but not from Jumpoff Lookout.

SEE ALSO

- Wendy Warren: Lo*okout Stories*, this book

- Splawn, A. J.: *Kamiakin*. That's "Andrew Jackson Splawn", first Mayor of Yakima.

and author of the famous local history.

13

Pyramid Peak Lookout Site

5,715 Feet Elevation

T19N, R11E, Section 28

USFS lookout on the boundary between Mount Baker and
Wenatchee National Forests

King County

- ACCESS AT A GLANCE:

Off Highway 410 from either Greenwater or through the
Little Naches Basin Roads
to Pyramid Pass where the PCT crosses Cascade Crest
logging roads, between Chinook Pass to   the South and
Snoqualmie Pass to the north.
- **Lookout Style/Year:** An old style lookout was placed as early as
1923.
but more likely around 1938, removed or abandoned as early
as 1948
and could have lasted as long as 1969 in some form.
- **Facilities Present:** Some concrete and steel remains.
- **Nearby Lookout and Observation Sites:** Raven Roost Lookout
#7,
Arch Rock Shelter site, and Government Meadows. Great
view of Mt. Rainier to the west.
- **Fire Lookout Panorama Photo date:** 1929 and 1938.
- **Difficulty getting to the lookout site** on a scale of 1 (easy) to 5
(difficult): **3**

- Once there, difficulty to find the actual lookout remains on a scale of 1 (easy) to 5 (difficult): **2**

This lookout site is located in the headwaters of the Little Naches Basin, or roughly 28 miles east of Enumclaw along the Cascade Crest. The trailhead is accessed today over a seasonal logging road which links the Little Naches drainage with the Greenwater area.

Pyramid Peak is one of several "Pyramid" Peak names in Washington State. The Naches Pyramid Peak should not be mistaken for the Entiat Ranger District's Pyramid Mountain appearing in Ira Spring's book "Lookouts" (page 148). Another Pyramid Peak is located near Diablo Lake, in the Diablo-Ross Lake area (near the Canadian border). Our Pyramid Peak, at 5,715 feet in elevation has a thrilling view to the west, centered on Mt. Rainier's northeast corner.

Pyramid Peak is one of those jointly managed boundary lookouts that were common on the Naches District. This is because generally ranger districts are divided by well known ridge landmarks defining basins, so it is logical that a lot of dividing ridges have good viewpoints, thus lookouts.

SETTING

Pyramid Pass is not a recognized name for the pass through which Forest Road #1914 breaks across the Cascade Crest and becomes Forest Road #70 heading to Greenwater. Pyramid Pass is a notable landmark because it is also the break in the Cascade Crest Ridge where the PCT crosses the #1914 / #70 Road and wanders on north, around Pyramid Peak and on to Blowout Mountain, and thus on to Snoqualmie Pass. If you do not know Pyramid Pass and are looking for a good way to visit Government Meadow this is your route. Simply park at the pass, consider the various dispersed camping sites, and then wander down the Pacific Crest Trail to the south two miles to **Government Meadow**. The meadows is the well known historical location where the **Biles-Longmire Wagon Train** stopped in late October of 1853 to graze their livestock, and make preparations for the trip over the legendary cliffs and on down to Steilacoom. Chinook Pass Highway was not an option until 1931.

Between Chinook Pass and Snoqualmie Pass there is really only this one dependable vehicle access point to the PCT, a place that can be visited with relative ease driving a SUV. This is a good place to shuttle, feed, and marvel over PCT hikers as they trudge toward the final segment of the "Mexico to Canada" PCT foot race to oblivion. I'm not counting the Naches Pass 4x4 jeep trail suitable only for dedicated jeepers, and the often inaccessible Blow Out Mountain access point from Road #1913, the Road and not the date.

A lot of pioneer history is centered around **Government Meadows**, including" the 1841 visit by the **Wilkes Exploration Expedition**, the 1853 visit by **Theodore Winthrop**, the 53 wagons of the Longmire wagon train, road builder Allen, the notable absence of **George Brinton McClellan**, and the 1856 crossing of military and native troops as they jockeyed for advantage in what was to become the Territorial War of 1857. To that list also include the famous **Chief Kamiakin**, mountain men **Andy Burge and John Edgar** and a few other scattered pioneer wagons, cattle drives, horse drives, adventurers, natives, traders, trappers, and others who simply forgot to check in or sign the register, which didn't exist.

I should also mention that on many random days during the summer Pyramid Pass Road may host 10 to 50 vehicles including many logging trucks, traveling both ways between Greenwater and the mouth of the Little Naches Basin. Technically the pass roadway, and several miles both ways is a private logging road and the gate, lurching innocently in the ditch on both sides of the pass, is occasionally locked for a few hours or days for the loggers to establish their domain. Just don't say I didn't tell you!

Lost Cannon (The popular myth): It is worth remembering that in the 1850s the Territorial Army, explorers, and road builders crossed and re-crossed Naches Pass many times, dragging, packing, or just generally carrying under their arms a cannon or two on each trip, primarily to confuse later amateur historians. As the army was in the habit of leaving cannons of one sort or another all over the territory, it can only be surmised that they left at one, or possibly two, or even perhaps three or more well known locations no one knew about. Government Meadow would have been an ideal place to bury a cannon for later generations to search for; sort of the Geo Cache of the 1850's. In any case, rumors built up over the years as they will, egged on by 5 or 6, or even more perhaps, firsthand sightings and "actually seens", even though it probably didn't exist. In any case, the cannon or cannons were never found and it remains only for some lucky retired person with a metal detector to visit the meadow, just as I have done or eventually plan to do, and otherwise diligently not find said cannon, "Said" being code which all cannon hunters well know means, "we know it's there, all we have to do is find it and dig it up". Well, until then, I'm coming down on the side that still believes in hope, big foot, and lost cannons. However, sometimes leveler heads prevail, as follows:

Academic clarification of the above fanciful discussion, *(The FACTS)*

The term, "Territorial Army" does not match an actual group that existed at the time. There were two separate military organizations that crossed over Naches Pass in the Mid 1850s.

1. U.S. Army (October 1855) Lt. Slaughter / Cpt. Maloney -they did not bring a cannon with federal troops.

2. Washington Territory Volunteers (June 1856) Lt. Col. Shaw and DeLacy - they did not bring a cannon with citizen soldiers.

All other military entries, federal and Territorial, into the Yakima Valley (i.e. Haller, Rains, Nesmith, Wright, Sheridan, Garnett, Steptoe, etc.) all came from The Dalles over the Simcoe Mountains.

(Added academia note: "There are a few other lookout books already in the marketplace, therefore, you probably don't want to be known as the "inaccurate" one.")

GETTING THERE

- (1) and (2)) Old unmarked trail from informal Pyramid Pass North Pacific Crest Trailhead accessed   f r o m either Green Water or the Little Naches Road west of Cliffdell.

- (3) Entering **Pyramid Pass** from Government Meadow to the South

    - or Blowout Mountain to the north

    - by way of the Pacific Crest National Scenic Trail #2000.

(1) From the east side: Past Whistlin' Jack Lodge and on up the Little Naches Drainage and,

(2) From the west side of the Cascades on Road #70 near Greenwater, Washington, a small Mountain community on State Route 410: The Pyramid Pass area offers a number of good dispersed camping spots. It is also the best point to hike south to Government Meadow which is a good place to rendezvous with PCT hikers. Pyramid Pass also offers good hiking trail access onto the PCT running in either direction, and a wonderful place to get flattened by a logging truck.

TO PYRAMID PASS

- (1) BY WAY OF private log haul Little Naches Road #1914 which extends from the end of the #1900 Little Naches Road west from Highway 410, near the Little Naches Campground. After about 15 miles on the #1900 Road the pavements ends and the #1914

gravel route extends to the right, and around 5 miles later crosses the Pacific Crest Trail at the point the road crosses the Cascade Crest and wonders on West, disguised as the #70 Road to Greenwater.

- (2) OR FROM Greenwater off Highway 410 on Forest Road #70 (700) to Pyramid Pass, which is generally the location of Pacific Crest Trail (PCT) North and South trailheads. From Greenwater travel east on Highway 410, past the local fire station (on the left) a mile or so out of town and watch for Forest Road #70 (or #7000). You will follow a paved portion of this road that eventually turns to gravel at about the point the Forest Service has given up on signing. And why there isn't just one road number all the way from Highway410 to Highway 410 isn't all that puzzling as national forests and counties converge here. This road number change will work against us finding Pyramid Pass in an hour or so, but well get there, right. Leave it to say that this road is the connecting road to the Little Naches Road 1914 coming from the east side of highway 410. Using a map, keep driving uphill and attempt to find either Pyramid Pass or Road #7080 which will take you there. Or follow a logging truck, or ask someone else who is lost, or just keep looking as the pass is found by driving generally "uphill".

And from either direction at Pyramid Pass:

A map is essential to this segment of your trip. Once you get to Pyramid Pass you are near the Pyramid Peak Trail, but the route to the North PCT Pyramid Peak Trailhead is a challenge to find though you're just about there. From the pass you may notice the PCT. One would think the PCT is well signed but quite simply, it is not. But then, only a few thousand "through hikers" venture this way each year on the almost final leg of their 2,642.4 mile trek. The southern extension dodges into some trees on the upper south side of the road and the northern direction drops down off the road bank to the north, remarkably similar to a cow path. You may be lucky enough to actually find some PCT signing on either side, but don't count on it or look for remarkably obscure signing which makes sense only after you know where you are, much like life.

You can follow the PCT Trail about ½ mile north, or take #1914-787 Spur Road north parallel to the PCT. After a great view of Mt. Rainier to the west, continue on a short ways and you will notice an unmapped spur (stub?) road running up the hill to the left. Walk or drive up the hill 50 yards to a nice, unattended trailhead with cryptic, PCT related signing. Camp or park here and follow the PCT Trail out of the trailhead approximately 100 feet north, watching for an unsigned, seldom used, and almost invisible Pyramid Peak trail on the right. That is the mythical, abandoned, unsigned, unmaintained, and often un-noticed trail which, within 2 miles will take you up to the old lookout. If you go 100 yards north on the PCT and can't find the trail, return to the trailhead and try again. If you stay on the PCT and skirt Pyramid Peak on the west side you will progress to the north side where the PCT wanders on north and east to Blow Out Mountain on the way to Snoqualmie Pass. It's logical that the peak trail comes out here on the north side also but logic, coupled with Time may have mostly obscured this route.

- (3) From Blowout Mountain or Government Meadow: You can also approach Pyramid Pass on the PCT south from Blowout Mountain or traveling north from Government Meadow but these routes require extra driving and hiking. However, if you wish to visit Blowout Mountain or Government Meadow they are both interesting features. At Government Meadows you can commune with History and at Blowout Mountain you can look north to the vicinity of Snoqualmie Pass.

From Blowout Mountain hike south on the PCT about four miles to Pyramid Pass and from Government Meadows hike north on the PCT about two miles to Pyramid Pass. Blowout Mountain can be accessed from the #1913 Road, off the #1900 Little Naches Road. The #1913 Road can be challenging in season: Cross the Little Naches River on a concrete bridge and clatter up the hill to the crest near Blowout. Blowout Mountain is often purported to be a lookout site but without evidence that I have been able to locate. See the discussion on Blowout Mountain in the Spiral Butte, #24 section.

Government Meadow is on the PCT and the historic Naches Pass Wagon Road, now the Naches Pass Jeep Trail and you can reach it from any number of PCT access points to the south including Chinook Pass, Raven Roost, Louisiana Saddle, and the Little Naches Jeep Road # 684. On either route, your "1 inch to the mile" map can help you get there.

SEE ALSO

- Gossett Gretta: Pyramid Peak, p. 480

- Gossett, Gretta: regarding the Lost cannon a few miles south at Government Meadows, p. 441

- Spring, Ira: "Lookouts", p. 152: A different "Pyramid Mountain"

- Hiler, Mike, *A History of Naches Pass*, Signpost Magazine, July, 1989

- Hiler, Mike. *A History of the PCT*, Signpost Magazine August, 1988

- Miles, Jo N: Miles, *Kamiakin Country* by, Caxton Press, 2017

14

Quartz Mountain Lookout Site

6,290 Feet Elevation

T18N, R14E, Section 3

Kittitas County

Cle Elum Ranger District in the head of Taneum Creek Basin

- ACCESS AT A GLANCE:

From Ellensburg or Cle Elum, nineteen or so total miles on the Taneum Forest Road #33
- and Manashtash Forest Road #31.
- **Lookout style and year:** Possibly older lookout style or tent platform 1929 – 1938.
- newer cabin on a 40' pole tower 1938 – mid 1960s.
The adjacent guard station, according to the panorama, was in place by 1934.
- **Facilities Present:** Pieces of bent steel footings.
- **Nearby Lookout and Observation Sites:** Big Bald Mountain Lookout Site #9,
- Frost Mountain Lookout site on the Cle Elum Ranger District, 3 miles east,
- and Lookout Point, on the Cle Elum District 4 miles northwest of Quartz Mountain.
- **Fire Lookout Panorama Photo date:** 1929, 1934, 1938.
- **Difficulty getting to the lookout site** on a scale of 1 (easy) to 5 (difficult): **4**

- Once there, difficulty to find the actual lookout remains on a scale of 1 (easy) to 5 (difficult)**: 1**

Q uartz Mountain Lookout site is located along Manastash Ridge north of the Little Naches River mouth, and is managed by the Cle Elum Ranger District. Motorbikes, horses or hikers can access Quartz Mountain by way of Taneum Road #33 from Thorp, WA or Manastash Road #31 from Ellensburg. The lower Taneum Road system is suitable for passenger cars but the upper sections can be challenging, particularly in spring and fall, or when annual road maintenance has not been completed. Don't worry about blowdown as the numerous jeepers in the area will have cleared the roads to Quartz by early summer.

All lookouts have outstanding views and are worth the trip, but the Quartz view is stunning and unique. From this old lookout peak one can see 360 degrees all over the south central Cascades. Binoculars are necessary to pick out the distant peaks way to the north with prominent peaks in full view. Of course Rainier and Adams poke up appropriately. Blowout Mountain, Pyramid Peak, Raven Roost, Shellrock Peak. Dome Peak all peeking over closer ridges for a surprising bonus. Quartz Mountain also offers good views over Manastash Ridge to the north and south. The Naches Ranger District 1 inch per mile *Fireman's Map* is a good resource for visiting the lookouts in this book, but the Cle Elum Ranger District 1 inch to the mile *Fireman's Map* is essential for visiting Quartz Mountain, as well as Bald Mountain Lookout #9 and Pyramid Peak Lookout #13. If you have the "Peak Finder" app on your iPhone this is one spot where that curious phone app suddenly makes sense.

The Yakima Valley Museum photo file on Civil Conservation Corps Projects" shows workers pioneering the Quartz Mountain Road from Cle Elum in 1936, but of course, the lookout buildings could have been constructed BR (before road). That road work was probably completed by the Ellensburg CCC Camp #939 while Camp #932, over in the Naches Basin was working on the Raven Roost Road

#1902. In light of the Depression it is unlikely that a camp had more than one road building caterpillar. Lookout access was always an important criteria for the placement and management of the lookouts, and even today, long after the lookout era wound down, access is an important reason some lookouts are gone and others remain. However, road maintenance funds dried after the "Big timber Cut" years ended around 1980. After that some lookouts like Jumpoff (lookout #4), which were at one time easy to visit in a standard sedan, became challenging even to jeeps and trailbikes.

If you visit Quartz, and have the time, don't forget to summit Frost Mountain, a few miles down the road from Quartz. It is anyone's guess why two lookouts were located so close together, perhaps it was a "road location" thing. Frost Mountain Lookout Site is an easy side trip off access spur Road #3100 – 123 by way of the #120 Spur. Stay on the #31 Road to go on to Quartz Mountain.

Another side trip, worth the minimal effort is **Taneum Lake** from the Taneum Lake trailhead, a few miles before you reach the lookout. A local lookout anomaly is "**Lookout Point**, a few miles NW from Quartz Mountain which never, as far as I know, hosted a lookout. Other local "Lookout Points" proliferate across the state.

SETTING

The Quartz mineral in the crystalline form is common in the Naches and Cle Elum Ranger Districts. This mineral scatter extends from Russell Ridge on north to Red Top Mountain Lookout (in Swauk Pass area) and back and forth between east and west. Quartz is a rough indicator of hard rock gold so in the prospectors heyday, everyone knew what it was and got excited if they found some.

GETTING THERE

Lower stretches of Manastash and Taneum Roads progresses from paved roads with turnouts to roads suitable only for SUV or pickup, and on to the last few miles of challenging general use gravel road. The final ¼ mile is suitable for only dedicated 4x4 jeep access but by that time you are ready to stretch your legs, so be it. Other road systems, interpreted by Chief Boyardee will also get you to the lookout from Cle Elum, WA but require intimate studies with a map, magnifying glass, and if possible, someone familiar with the topography.

(1) FROM Highway 90 near Thorp on the Taneum Road #33 Road system and then

Road # 3330, to the #3120 and onto the 4x4 Road #3100 (#31) to Quartz Mountain.

(2) OR from the Manastash Road #31 to 4x4 Road #3100 and on to Quartz Mountain.

The hike in from Bald Mountain is heavily convoluted

by a mythical 4x4 trail system of some 19 miles

and is recommended only as self inflicted torture based on uncertainty.

(1) Highway 90 between Ellensburg and Cle Elum: Between Ellensburg and Cle Elum, along the Interstate 90, a small basin whistle stop, and now including an additional truck stop by the name of Thorp, is displayed prominently on freeway exit signs. Exit at Thorp and follow the signs to the Taneum Basin, several miles to the southwest. The Taneum Basin Road #33 is paved to the Ice Water Campground.

Progress past the Ice Water Campground and turn left onto Forest Road #33. From here you will drive over forest road(s) 19 miles to the lookout, throwing in a final walk in case your vehicle is not up to the challenging final climb. Eventually, turn right onto Road #31 and continue west. The first part of this drive is suitable for a SUV or two wheel drive pickup but the final four miles get just a tad bit more challenging, requiring some rock throwing and careful puddle jumping. The final 1/4 mile of this road climbs sharply up to the lookout on a rocky 4x4 jeep road, suitable only for dedicated 4x4 enthusiast.

(2) This route may be more appropriate when approaching from Ellensburg. Leave town on the Umptanum Road from the south end of town heading west. Travel on Umptanum Creek Road after a hard west and progress about 3 miles from town. Following signs, turn onto the Manashtash Forest Road # 31, driving generally northwest. The bottom section of this road is paved and meanders through an extended country residence area, somewhat unique in Eastern Washington. After Several miles up the paved road regresses to forest gravel, some washboard, and numerous rock spots that may be more appropriate for coming down than going up.

The lower segments of this trip, like the Taneum route are suitable for pickups and SUVs but expect rocky sections, and drive slow and easy to avoid tire damage. Sometime after passing the Taneum Road #33, on the right, progress on toward the lookout on the #31 Road. The last four miles of this road are a bit more challenging, and the last ¼ mile requires dedicated equipment. I suggest parking and walking on to the top, binoculars in hand.

SEE ALSO

- Big Bald Lookout #9

- Gossett, Gretta: Beyond the Bend, Quartz Mountain, p. 486

The History of Wilderness and Visiting Wilderness sites.

Wilderness trail travel involves hiking or horseback.

Wilderness sites are often remote and requires a multiple day trip.

Review the "Wilderness Travel" suggestions in the appendix

Travel in small groups,

National Forest "Wild Area" and "Primitive Area" designations go back a ways, but "Wilderness" with a capital W was Federally designated in 1964 when the system was created from large pieces of federal lands, to be managed for primitive types of recreation where the landscape is free from the trace and activities of mankind. Wilderness trails are for foot power. Mechanical transport is prohibited.

Many of the old lookouts were located in areas now Wilderness but few of those stations remain and the sites are now managed for their educational or historical values within an area where the traces of man are minimized. Trail access is the only way to those old remote viewpoints. For those reasons, these are the most challenging sites to visit and though they generally offer a great view and a good place to have lunch, the mountain tops they occupy are poor camping spots: exposed, with irregular surface, and lacking access to water. For those reasons I suggest that an overnight stay at an old Wilderness site be found, if needed, where you do not dominate the site and that you reserve your curiosity about actual lookout stations for the few locations outside Wilderness where the buildings remain, hopefully in some manageable context. Visiting an old lookout station is quite an experience but let's support the Wilderness values in areas that are difficult to visit and impractical to maintain and reserve our enthusiasm for lookouts where our efforts serve a broader visitor base.

SEE ALSO

- Hiler, Mike: *The History of Wilderness*, Signpost Magazine May, 1985
- Appendix D, *Wilderness ethics*

Goat Rocks Wilderness Lookouts

LITTLE BALD
MTN
LOOKOUT

ELEV
5996

E. BROWN

15

Bear Creek Mountain
Lookout Site

7,336 feet Elevation

T12N, R12E, Section 17

South Goat Rocks Wilderness near Gilbert Peak

- ACCESS AT A GLANCE:

Wilderness trail access at Section 3 Lake Trailhead, west of Rimrock Lake
at the west end of Pine Grass Ridge. Final 2 miles of access road may be difficult to negotiate.
- **Lookout Style/Year:** Older style building 1930's to 1960 or so.
- **Facilities Present:** Evidence of concrete foundation remains.
- **Nearby Lookout and Observation Sites**: Round Mountain #7, Darland Mountain #2.
- **Fire Lookout Panorama Photo date:** 1934.
- **Difficulty getting to the lookout site** on a scale of 1 (easy) to 5 (difficult): **4**
- **Once there, difficulty to find the actual lookout remains** on a scale of 1 (easy) to 5 (difficult): **1**

Bear Creek Mountain Lookout was located within what is now the Goat Rocks Wilderness on Bear Creek Mountain. This site is accessed from Section 3 Lake Trailhead over Trail #1130. The drive to the trailhead from Naches is approximately 2 hours, and the hike of three miles will take approximately 4 hours, round trip with photos and sightseeing. The trail climbs steeply from the final junction on trail #1130A but it is not a particularly difficult hike, even for children and the alpine setting is rewarding. When did you last hike where you could follow official rock cairns?

The ground around the old lookout site is now scattered with glass and nails, a telephone line strand of #9 wire roughly follows the trail to the site. The outhouse is apparently gone, and obligatory trash dumps, if any, used by the lookouts are not visible or evident. Concrete foundation blocks indicate the dimensions of the structure that sat on the ground. There was no tower at this site because of the unobstructed, open alpine mountain top view.

SETTING

Section 3 Lake is little more than a tadpole pond, and it was there, in the 1970s that two young campers imagined they saw a big foot type monster stalking their tent in the hours of darkness. The Yakima County Sheriff's deputy and forest patrol **Tom Dekkar** were unable to locate the curious beast.

Arvile Willard served here around 1942, as well as, apparently, Jumpoff Lookout and Mt. Adams Lookout in the early 40s.

GETTING THERE

- FROM Highway 12 by way of paved County Road1#1200 near Rimrock Lake
    - FS gravel Road #1260, and on to FS Gravel Road #1205,
- AND forest gravel Road #1204 ending at Section 3 Lake Trailhead
- AND on to Wilderness hiking Trail #1130A by way of #1130 Trail.

Bear Creek Mountain Wilderness trail, although located at the end of a rugged gravel (you wish) road, is one of the most popular hikes on the Naches District, and with good reason. This road can be snow covered in early season, muddy at midsummer, rutted in late summer, and snowed in all winter. Summertime here may be a frame of mind.

From Highway 12 near Rimrock Lake turn onto the #1200 loop road east or west of Rimrock Lake. Two miles east of Clear Lake, take the Forest Service gravel Cold Creek #1205 Road. This will take you up and onto the Pinegrass Ridge, a large tableland the Forest Service attempted unsuccessfully to turn into a tree plantation in the 1950s. Follow the #1205 to the #1204 Road which takes you to the Section 3 Lake Trailhead, accessing the trail to Bear Creek Mountain In case you didn't read above, the final 2 miles of the Trailhead Road can be difficult to negotiate with a standard vehicle, or even a standard high clearance pick-up so come with the thought in mind that you may need to park a mile or two before the actual trailhead, in the shade, and walk a short ways to the bulletin board. Of course, a two mile walk, round trip equals four miles and requires another hour or so.

There are a number of other ways to get to, or from **Pine Grass Ridge**. In the Tieton South Fork , off Road #1000 you can take the Pine Tree Road #1241 to the #1204 Road or from Gray Creek take the #1000 – 750 Spur to Road #1241 and on to the #1204 Road to Section 3 Lake. Or, however you get on Pinegrass Ridge you need to find Road #1204 and follow it to the western dead end at Section 3 Lake (In Section 3!).

SEE ALSO

- *Wilderness camping etiquette* and *leave no trace* (Woodsy Owl) guidelines, Appendix D

16

Round Mountain Lookout Site

5,971 Feet Elevation

T13N, R12E, Section 9

Goat Rocks Wilderness overlooking White Pass Highway
South of White Pass

- ACCESS AT A GLANCE:

Off White Pass Highway 12 at Clear Lake and on to the
Round Mountain Road
some 4 miles to the trailhead, suitable for those exercise
challenged though generally uphill.

- Lookout Style/Year: Older style lookout on tower, 1935 – 1976,

- possibly replaced with a newer style, 1950 or 1951.

- Facilities Present: Tower foundation – original outhouse, hidden
among the trees.

- Nearby Lookout and Observation Sites: Bear Creek Mountain
#15, Spiral Butte
Fire Observation Site #24, views into this area off the Pacific
Crest Trail south of White Pass,
particularly on the western portion of Twin Peaks Trail
#1144 connecting the PCT
to Round Mountain, and, the short climb from near the Clear
Lake Spillway
to the crest of **Kamiakin Butte** over an unmarked user trail.

- Fire Lookout Panorama Photo: None that I know of. Surprising as this was once a key lookout.
- Difficulty getting to the lookout site on a scale of 1 (easy) to 5 (difficult): **2**
- Once there, difficulty to find the actual lookout remains on a scale of 1 (easy) to 5 (difficult): **1**

Round Mountain is located west of Clear Lake in the Tieton Basin. This prominent peak overlooks Rimrock Lake and into the Cascade Crest at White Pass. Good views open to the south into Goat Rocks, and to the north into the William O. Douglas Wilderness. From this point a number of other lookouts could be triangulated, including Bear Creek Mountain, Jumpoff (in the distance east), Tumac, and others.

The Goat Rocks Wilderness hike to Round Mt is about three climbing miles from the trailhead, pretty much "UP" the whole way. This day hike is suitable for families as it offers good resting spots and outstanding scenery along the way. Although the trip is not particularly challenging, even for well trained children, you can make a shorter day trip by just driving to the trailhead to enjoying the scenery and commute with a true mountain spring, albeit unfiltered. Actually, the whole east side of Round Mt is a series of springs that dump into Clear Creek and thus, Clear Lake, a reservoir that takes part in storing and distributing water to downstream irrigators.

There are plenty of campgrounds at the west end of Rimrock Lake (Clear Lake) and some dispersed camping spots in the general area. Sometimes in the fall huckleberries are scattered lightly over the northeast side of Round Mountain but don't count on it or expect to fill a gallon jug, even when a few berries dare show their shiny little faces before being gobbled up. The climb from near the Clear Lake spillway to the top of **Kamiakin Butte** might be as rewarding as the climb to Round Mountain, only much shorter and without the extra driving.

Round Mountain was one of the last Tieton Ranger District lookout stations to be destroyed. It was used primarily in times of high fire danger, and during periods of lightning activity. The old style 20 foot tower was removed in 1976. Remains of this lookout site include concrete pillars with iron hangers, profuse glass and nails resulting from the lookout removal, a few piles of the remains of old batteries, foundation, and traces of an adjacent barn or shed. The standard, official, and historically unique lookout toilet is still in relatively good shape but hard to find back in the trees.

I can remember the day the Round Mountain Lookout tower was reluctantly dynamited to the ground by powder monkey and packer **Bill Rennie**. Listening to the progress of his mostly futile effort over a Forest Service radio from my Wilderness camp at McCall Basin I was, strangely, amused by Bill's periodic calls back to the station and almost doubled over with laughter at the replies of **Walt Tokarczyk**, his puzzled "Big Boss" supervisor. The tension was heightened because I could easily hear the powder "boom" from my camp at the Basin, followed a short time later by the squawk of the keyed radio mic and Bill's pronouncement of "it's still standing......
Walt", followed some 30 seconds later by Walt's puzzling reply. I have no idea why, but I have the feeling that we were all sharing some deeply ingrained sympathy for the underdog lookout tower, constructed with much effort by Arnie Arneson as we silently cheered the lookout for it's efforts to defy gravity and the progress represented by destroyed lookouts everywhere.

The Round Mountain Trailhead is a good place for photos and picnicking. Even if you only travel a short distance on the trail you will be rewarded with outstanding scenery. The four hour round trip hike offers great views into the White Pass. Dogs seem to love this hike for some reason?

Known firefighters who worked at Round Mt are almost too numerous to list. Bob Heikel of Moses Lake served there (1950?) 1951 – 53 (brother of El Heikel, see Goat Peak Lookout 17#). George

Parks served 1942, Rollin Yost 43, Bruce Morris, Glen Blevens of Bellingham served1956 - 58 and Bob Messer (of Yakima) was the last "Lookout of Record" at this very picturesque and classic old lookout, perched on the tower in paradise.

SETTING

It is logical to assume that an old trail went this way by Twin Peaks before the White Pass Highway was built or that a trail connected Clear Creek with the Cascade Crest at White Pass. This route would have provided access to mountain goat habitat, to the obsidian quarry near Elk Pass, and on to the west side at Big Bottom (Packwood). These were "Mountain Natives", traders who speared their fish in the manner described in **William O. Douglas** classic of this area, *Of Men and Mountains.* Hiking this area without first researching the area through the Douglas book is almost like trying to run before you can walk; fruitless, and through the historical looking glass of the local area.

If you are interested in the unique horse packing history in the Naches area you'll enjoy the short film clip by Forest Ranger Arnie Arneson which records (celebrates) the construction of the Round Mountain lookout. This home movie, transferred to a VHS tape by the Forest Service, illustrates the packing of long timbers to the lookout site on Round Mountain by trusty pack mules working in tandem. The individual beams were packed to the peak using two packhorses connected with a unique swivel packsaddle.

Near the White Pass North PCT trailhead is the location of what some say is the now dilapidated cabin of Trapper and mountain man Hulbert Beebe, whose suspected alias of D. B. Cooper has made him a quiet, thought growing myth of these mythical mountains, **Bob Delaware Cooper** not withstanding.

GETTING THERE

- (1) FROM Highway 12 by way of paved County Road #1200 near Rimrock Lake

   TO Forest Road #1200-530 west of Clear Lake and on to the trailhead at road end

   BY WAY OF Wilderness Trail #1144 and on to the lookout.

- (2) OR off the Pacific Crest Trail #2000 south of White Pass (highway 12)

   BY WAY OF Twin Peaks Trail #1144 traveling east.

(1) The Round Mountain site is accessed by taking Round Mountain Road #1200-830 from Clear Lake to the Round Mt Trailhead at Cedar Springs and then on Trail #1144 to near the peak where you will climb to the lookout on the lookout spur Trail #1144A to the lookout site. The lower mile of this trail is an old logging road that had some motorized use until it was re-legislated into Wilderness in 1984.

The trip begins along Highway 12. Drive west from Naches or east from Packwood. At the Clear Lake turnoff on Forest Road #1200, turn south. Drive by the campground entrance and YMCA Camp Dudley (formerly named Camp Kamiakin). On a clear day you will see a remarkable view of Goat Rocks over Clear Lake. Drive on one mile to spur road #830 on the right. The Round Mountain road climbs steadily for five miles to the trailhead. As you approach the trailhead you will start to see remarkable views back toward Rimrock Lake and Clear Lake. Drive on to the trailhead where good parking is available.

(2) You may also hike to Round Mountain on the Pacific Crest Trail #2000 from the White Pass South Trailhead, by way of the west Twin Peaks Trail #1144. The entire trip to White Pass and back to the Round Mountain trailhead is a long day and not recommended if you do not have plenty of time. However, the views are worth being late. A shuttle might be considered to allow for a longer day hike

SEE ALSO:

- Directions to Tumac Mountain Lookout #20 from White Pass North PCT Trailhead.

William O. Douglas
Wilderness Lookout Sites

17

American Ridge (Goat Peak) Lookout Site

6,473 Feet Elevation

T17N, R13E, Section 30

William O. Douglas Wilderness

Ridge peak between Bumping Road and Highway 410

- ACCESS AT A GLANCE:

Wilderness trails from several trailheads off Highway 410 west of Whistlin' Jack Lodge
OR paved Bumping Lake Road #1800.
- **Lookout Style/Year:** Older style lookout with hip style roof
Perhaps something in the 1920s but 1933 to 1968 was more official for the station
- **Facilities Present:** Evidence of concrete foundations.
- **Nearby Lookout and Observation Sites:** Miner's Ridge Lookout #6, and the
Bumping Lake overlook at the end of forest Chipmunk Road #1802.
- **Fire Lookout Panorama Photo date**: 1934.
- **Difficulty getting to the lookout site** on a scale of 1 (easy) to 5 (difficult): **4**
- **Once there, difficulty to find the actual lookout remains** on a scale of 1 (easy) to 5 (difficult): **3**

A merican Ridge Lookout site is located along the backbone of American Ridge at Goat Peak. Because there is another lookout in Washington State named Goat Peak (near Easton, Gossett), this lookout is formally called American Ridge Lookout. Local use of the name "Goat Peak" however is common.

The American Ridge Lookout Station was constructed in 1933 (or 34?) (Gossett and USDA Inventory). The lookout storage shelter was placed in 1934. The featured picture in Ira Spring's *Lookouts, Fire Watchers of the Cascades and Olympics* indicates that the 1934 model was of the later style hip roof design. A toilet (or storage building) was located below to the South. A prominent spring a mile or two to the west near the ridge top and identified on most local maps supplied water, transported daily in a backpack. Most lookouts had nearby springs, but still, it was hard work transporting water up to the lookout in a bladder backpack affair. Throw in chopping and transporting firewood and you have some idea of the fun of the whole thing.

American Ridge begins at the junction of the American and Bumping Rivers and climbs westward to the Cascade Crest by way of Goat Peak. The native campsite at this river junction and other evidence in the area leave little doubt this old ridge trail (running 27 miles from its lowest point to the junction with the Pacific Crest Trail #2000 near American Lake) was once familiar to native residents. Later, prospectors, sheepherders, trappers, and Wilderness Rangers trudged this spectacular ridge.

Lookouts: Pat Ford of Goose Prairie served on Goat Peak in 1944, Leo (Scotty) Campbell in 1947?, El Heikel 1954, and Bill Quist of Yakima in 1962.

SETTING

Goat Peak perches on the spine of American Ridge, between the Bumping and American Rivers. At one time this ridge was probably an island between glaciers. The terminal moraine in the Bumping is still visible just below the dam. Long and rugged, American Ridge is distinguished by great views and occasional springs. In the early 1900s domestic sheep bands and their trusty herders roamed these slopes, particularly at Big Basin, west of Goat Peak. Tom Fife working a trap line along this ridge trapped lynx here early in the century. Now the ridge is almost abandoned by all but elk, a few mountain goats and the occasional hunter, hiker or horseback riders.

The American Ridge Lookout wood stove chimney is visible in the 1934 Panorama photo. The old photographic panorama is often the only remaining hard evidence of what was actually at the site.

GETTING THERE

- (1) FROM Hells Crossing on Highway 410 by way of Trail #958C.

- (2) OR FROM the paved Bumping Road #1800 at Goat Creek Trailhead on Trail #959.

- (3) OR FROM American Ridge Trailhead off the Bumping Road #1800

ON the American Ridge Trail #958.

- (4) Or Bushwhacking from the Chipmunk Road #1802.

I won't include the access to American Ridge Lookout site from the Pacific Crest Trail as you can technically get to Goat Peak from anywhere in the world. The most obvious route, up the American Ridge from the American Ridge Trailhead actually isn't the most popular route. More direct, and a toss-up as to which is preferred are two aerobic hikes, one from Goat Creek Trailhead along the Bumping Lake Road and the other the Goat Peak Trailhead at Hells Crossing along Highway 410. Naturally, anyone who wants to make their hike to Goat Peak more interesting can simply depart any of the numerous other American Ridge access trails and find their way to the peak using a good forest map.

(1) From Hells Crossing, off Highway 410 on the Goat Peak Trail #958C. Hells Crossing is 6 miles west of the Bumping Lake Road turnoff on Highway 410 (west of Whistln' Jack Lodge). There is lots of parking here, and usually more cars as a lot of other hikers will be hiking the Pleasant Valley loop Trail #999, along American River departing from the same trailhead. There is also good developed camping at Hells Crossing Campground for those who want to spend a night or visit the huge Larch at Pleasant Valley Campground. The Goat Peak Trail hike, like the one on the other side of the ridge which departs from Goat Creek Trailhead, is an aerobic climb, not impossible but rewarding for those who like some great views and physical challenge.

(2) From the Bumping Road at Goat Creek Trailhead on the Goat Creek Trail #959: The lookout is about 6 miles of aerobic hiking. Camping is available at Cougar Flats Developed Campground almost directly across the Bumping Road from the Goat Creek Trailhead.

(3) Hiking up the American Ridge Trail #958 from the trailhead near the Bumping Road turnoff: The American Ridge Trailhead is located about one half mile west from the American River Guard Station located near the turnoff onto the Bumping Lake Road. American Ridge Trailhead is a good shady place to park, and possibly camp if you have a "Trail Park" sticker. An unsigned outfitter guide trail connects the trailhead to the outfitter guide camp near the Guard Station. Those who want a more leisurely day can rent ponies from the accommodating outfitter who camps near the guard station on the site of the old, and now departed American River Lodge.

Depart on American Ridge Trail #959 and hike 8 miles west, climbing up the ridge to the old lookout Site. This is an interesting trail as if flips back and forth over the ridge, giving the trail traveler alternate views of both the Bumping Basin and the American River Basin.

(4) The fourth route requires some bushwhacking and orienteering, as well as old fashioned pioneering from the Forest Road #1802 which climbs American Ridge from a point about two miles past the guard station: Turn off Highway 410 at the Bumping Lake Road junction and progress 2 miles to the west. The Chipmunk Road #1802 to the North is the only logging road off the Bumping Lake Road. Even if you are not hiking to the lookout, you will get some remarkable views along this road, particularly at the end where you can bushwhack on up to American Ridge trail, a challenging 1 or 2 mile hike depending on where the crow starts and how the crow flies.

At the end of the road you can easily find a place to park and hike on up the hill through rough country, angling somewhat north and generally uphill, following your compass (you know, that thing that doesn't use batteries) working with your map to "Search out" the American Ridge Trail. Good news, as long as you are hiking UP HILL you are heading for the American Ridge Trail. Don't forget, the real trick with bushwhacking is finding your way BACK to your vehicle, thus GPS.

A somewhat easier route is a couple miles back down from the road end, above the switchback in section 22 which you will only know about when you get there. Return back downhill to a point you determine is closer to the American Ridge Trail, in the vicinity of old uphill logging spurs inadvertently indicated on maps as closed spur #1802-645. Parking here at the road edge is no problem but be sure to put a rock under your back tires, or, look for a wide spot with a plethora of suitable scotch rocks that earlier hunters and visitors have put under THEIR tires. Then you will know you are close.

Your copy of the District Trail Guide, "Getting Lost", as well as no visible signs and little use on these spurs might frustrate your efforts, but you know the American Ridge Trail is up there near the top somewhere and as long as you hike "north and up" you just might find it.

Remember, simply hike down if you get lost, in which case unplanned cross-country forays either into the American River or into the Bumping Basin will be long, steep, and a somewhat dangerous route for orienteering. If you are following a map, read the land closely, read your map closer, and if you like to sleep in your own bed at night, use a GPS to return to your vehicle, battery included.

Big Larch at Pleasant Valley: At Pleasant Valley Campground, along Highway 410 on the American River section, an extra large old growth Tamarack (Western Larch) resides on the river edge at the back of a campsite near the old CCC Shelter. It is not a National Champion but it does deserve recognition for the centuries it has graced the kingdom of large ant-hills and occasional anadromous salmon traveling to spawning grounds. Please treat the tree and the fish with respect.

SEE ALSO

- Nelson, Jack: *We Never Got Away*
- Spring, Ira*: Fire Watchers of the Cascades and Olympics* by Ira Spring, p. 160
- Gossett, Gretta: p. 468, (Goat Peak)
- Gossett, Gretta: American River Guard Station, p. 456
- Hiler, Mike*: Skiing American Ridge*, Signpost Magazine, October, 1986
- Hiler, Mike*: Names and Misnames on the Naches*,
- Landmarks Magazine Vol. IV, #s 3 & 4, No date.

18

Clover Springs Lookout Site

6,351 Feet Elevation

T16N, R13E, Section 22

Located just inside the William O. Douglas Wilderness near
Clover Springs

- ACCESS AT A GLANCE:

Multiple approaches off Highway 410, east and west of
Whistlin' Jack Lodge
by way of several different, rugged 4X4 jeep roads.

- Lookout Style/Year: Older temporary style lookout with firefinder: 1930s – 1960.

- Facilities Present: Rock foundation in poor shape, condition is
fragile.

- Nearby Lookout and Observation Sites: Little Bald Lookout #5.

- Fire Lookout Panorama Photo date: 1936.

- Difficulty getting to the lookout site on a scale of 1 (easy) to 5
(difficult): **4**

- Once there, difficulty to find the actual lookout remains on a
scale of 1 (easy) to 5 (difficult): **5**

Clover Springs is a high mountain meadow along the **natural
route** between the Nile Valley pastures and **Goose Prairie**.
Views into the Bumping Basin to the west, into the North Fork of
Rattlesnake Creek, north and south make this a good fire watch
location. Clover Springs, as an auxiliary viewpoint with some visual blank spots, in this case poor visibility into the east and south

basins. Perched on a side hill it was built simply to support Little Bald lookout one mile to the Northeast. The lookout guard stationed at Little Bald Lookout probably walked the distance daily or in association with lightening storms. No doubt Clover Springs was little more than a ground level structure that provided simple shelter.

Ira Spring, in his book *Lookouts* related that the Clover Springs site hosted a "tent and fire finder" used in conjunction with the Little Bald Mountain lookout station, Kresek indicates that an L-5 Lookout cabin was built here in the 1930's and removed in 1960. Forest Service records indicate this lookout was "proposed" in 1939. A separate 1948 Forest map indicates no lookout here. Both records may be wrong, or correct. The old "foundation" was not strongly built and evidence of this station is rather fragile and quickly fading.

The old Clover Springs lookout remains are somewhat difficult to locate. You will find it by climbing the 4x4 drive/trail several hundred yards south of the Clover Springs camping area. At the top of the hill, hike over the ridge into wilderness and walk back toward the meadows along this ridge. A few feet to the west you will notice an old, crumbling stone foundation approximately 10 feet by 10 feet. A nearby USGS "brass cap" benchmark will tell you when you are getting close.

Many of the old fire lookout sites in the Northwest were located at the edge of ridges or basins and did not have a compete view in all directions, even with a tower. Many lookout views were improved with the cutting of a few trees but if this didn't work area managers often constructed a nearby temporary viewpoint which filled in the visibility gaps and which were used during times of high fire danger or after lightening storms. This explains the close proximity of the Little Bald and Clover Springs lookout sites, on the Naches Ranger District. These two lookout sites together, both now abandoned, offered excellent, and full, views into the upper Naches River Basin(s).

SETTING

Clover Springs does offer remarkable views into rugged Wilderness but in the other three directions trees block any practical view, if views can be practical. The four wheel drive (4x4 jeep) **Nile Ridge Trail** runs from here back toward roads near Mud Springs and is an outstanding ridge top travel route, challenging for jeeps but suitable for mountain bike, horseback or hiking, in either direction. Please do not drive vehicles west off the established 4x4 road as cliffs define the western edge of this entire route. Observing the Wilderness boundary will help protect Wilderness values, and is a good way to avoid oblivion.

The Windy Ridge Trail, running west from Clover drops you into the heart of the William O. Douglas Wilderness. Don't forget, you'll have to climb back out of this hole from "**Diamond S Camp**" (Sinclair?) at the bottom where the old "**Whisky Stop**" **Trail** wanders back down toward the fabled Rattlesnake Creek toward McDaniel Lake.

Clover Springs (not the lookout) has long been a landmark camp and resting point along the old Nile Ridge Trail, once connecting the Nile community to Goose Prairie by way of **Mud Springs. "So Happy"** the local native chief during the Territorial war of 1856 camped at the Nile and was familiar with the trails western route. **Tom Fife, Ruben Root, Cap Simmons, and Tommy Amato** all knew this meadow and spring as a good place to camp and replenish water on their pack trips between Yakima and their Miner's Ridge claims. It must be remembered that when Tom Fife entered the Bumping there was no road up the Bumping River (Before Dam) and this overland route was the only, and therefore most direct way to access Goose Prairie from Yakima. In those days you had to be a packer to even visit Goose Prairie.

It was at Clover Springs that **Hindoo John's horse** was found wandering after his mysterious death in August 1896 (1889?), tending sheep on the other side of Mt. Aix. Legend tells us that **Zokseye,** a pioneer era native camped at Clover Springs when he departed into the mountains to "work" his secret gold claim. See The Mt Aix lookout #19 chapter "Setting" for more on the Hindoo John discussion.

From Clover Springs the Nile Ridge Trail drops northward to the Bumping River and Goose Prairie but this old (road to road) trail is almost forgotten today and gets little use. Flat Iron Lake, just a hop, skip, and jump to the east was once a prospecting center and you may find some old foundations there on the lake shore. This old trail does offer a possible downhill hike for those who arrange a shuttle from Goose Prairie, but this route traverses Wilderness and is not legal for mountain bikes or large groups. See the section below for a discussion about Flat Iron Lake and the Soda Springs hike. Don't' forget to visit the Soda Springs Campground Civil Conservation Corps shelter in almost original condition.

To the south from the Clover Spring the trail is now a challenging four-wheel route that leads back toward Mud Springs. Suitable only for dedicated narrow track, high centered, short wheel base four wheel drive vehicles with winches, this four wheel driveway is ideal for horseback, mountain bike, motorbikes or hiking. If you listen closely when the wind is howling up the Windy Ridge Trail you will hear Zokseye and **Tom Fife** exchanging stories about Hindoo John's lost mother load, aptly named "The Hindoo Horde". The Horde was most likely an exposure of the Iron Pyrite occasionally found in large chunks in Rattlesnake Creek. Iron Pyrite is also called "Fools Gold" and can be a rough indication of the real thing, or not. To protect drinking water quality for the City of Yakima a Rattlesnake Basin mineral withdrawal has excluded it from "Mineral Entry", a fancy way of saying you can't stake a gold claim.

A unique mountain peak landmark near here is worth mentioning: Old Scab Mountain located off the trail connecting Soda Springs trail to Flat Iron Lake. The journey to Old Scab requires some orienting and is ideal for those requiring something just a bit different in Wideness exploration.

GETTING THERE

    (1) FROM Cliffdell by way of Little Bald Lookout #5.

    (2) FROM the Nile area by way of Clover Springs Forest Road #1600.

    (3) FROM (or to) Mud Springs over 4x4 Driveway #1600-696 out of the Nile area.

    (4) HIKING FROM Goose Prairie on the Nile Ridge Wilderness Trail #974.

Clover Springs Lookout, and its companion Lookout Little Bald # 4, can be approached from several general routes. Those routes are: (1), from Cliffdell, by way of Little Bald Lookout, (2) From the Nile community by way of the #1600 Clover Springs Road, (3) By way of Mud Springs over the Nile Ridge 4x4 Way #1600-696, and (4) hiking up from Goose Prairie on the Nile Ridge Wilderness Trail #974. Other view points, places of interest, and optional return routes are also addressed below.

(1) From Cliffdell by way of Little Bald Lookout

Depart from Highway 410 west of Cliffdell on the Forest Road #1706 toward Bolder Cave. Cross the Naches River heading toward Boulder Cave and take a short left off the main road just before Camp Roganunda (and Boulder Cave). Continue to follow Forest Road #1706 eight miles up to the Clover Springs Road #1600, turn right and continue on 3 miles to the Little Bald Lookout Spur #1600-231.

From Little Bald turnoff the #1600 road deteriorates rapidly and most casual drivers will eventually give up on this road before they get to Clover Springs. Assuming that for some reason this road was accidently maintained a few days before you travel it, but generally not, expect rocky areas, washouts, occasional mud, and possible trees blocking the road. Note several stopping areas on your drive on to Clover, including Saddle Camp and the Flat Iron Lake Trailhead. A topographic map will help your orientation along this route(s) as signs may be down or difficult to read from the Little Bald turnoff.

You may encounter a domestic sheep herd along this road so be prepared to stop as the "woolies" find their way off the road, or more likely, as they doze in the road as they are prone to do in great numbers. In the 1920s over 200,000 sheep grazed the Naches and Tieton area but today only one band remains of this once thriving wool industry. This band of sheep is overseen by Forest Service range managers who rotate grazing cycles and paths to enhance forest resources. The Meadow Maggots droppings, also known as "sheep poop", will be returned to the soil which adds nutrients, and the grazing will clear back dense underbrush which increases fire danger. The best way to negotiate a car through a noisy bunch of sheep is to not get in a hurry (or be at one with the flowing mass of wool). Stay on Forest Road #1600 past the junction with Road #1706 and continue on west toward Clover Springs.

If you have a vehicle that isn't ready for 4x4 scouting but is able to navigate some bumps and rocks, you can drive up the road until your vehicle starts complaining. Park and hike the remaining distance. Saddle Camp is a suitable destination to reach by vehicle before the road worsens.

(2) By way of the Nile Community over Forest Roads

You may also drive in from the Nile area located off Highway 410, 18 miles west of Naches. Turn on the #1500 Road at **Eagle Rock Store (The Woodshed)** or turn into Nile area from the Upper Nile Loop Road (one mile east of Sprick Park, Nile Valley Days venue and several miles west of the Woodshed Restaurant. Progress into the Nile Community and turn west on the Clover Springs Forest Road #1600 near the Nile Community Center. This road is generally signed as the "Clover Springs Road.

As mentioned in the Little Bald Lookout # 5 discussion in this book: Three miles west on Road #1600 you will enter a large opening. This is a popular camping area which once housed the Nile Mill and before that the Little Fish Ranger Station. Around 1930 the Orr family operated a pine box mill here. Huge pine logs were skidded down to the mill over a rough skid-way. Later known as the Nile Railroad, this was simply a hauling skid where logs were pulled by surplus World War I vehicles with solid rubber tires. At one time a number of loggers and millers worked and lived here in a small, isolated community. The Little Fish Ranger Station was located here around the same time and the earliest 932nd Company Civil Conservation Corps (CCC) Camp was housed here during its first year of operation. No doubt Native Americans once camped near here also. Some also know this area as a winter elk feeding station.

And "what" you may ask, "is a Box Mill". Old growth pine which once graced Nile Flats, makes excellent packing boxes and the early Yakima fruit industry created an strong box demand. This mill did mill some building material for local residents, but the remote location, coupled with the cost of hauling, dictated boxes as the strongest practical market. The mill later moved to Naches, along the South Naches Highway just south of the Naches River.

As you leave the Little Fish area you will drive through a road cut bank of white chalky rock. This unique sedimentary rock strata is probably ancient volcanic ash deposited in ancient lake bed. You can also observe this large ash layer from the paved portion of Road #1500 in the lower Rattlesnake area. See Timberwolf Lookout #8 directions.

(3) Clover Springs Lookout #8 by way of the Mud Springs on the Nile Ridge 4x4 way

Approach Mud Springs (T16 N, R 14E, Section 32) from the Forest Road #1600. Now, locate the Nile Ridge 4x4 #1600-696 jeep driveway in the area of Mud Springs, a big disappointment as a spring, but so is living with Global Warming. From the point near where the sign to Spur #696 should be, tag along the 4x4 trail as it wanders north along the boundary ridge overlooking William O. Douglas Wilderness. This trail is challenging and some "side by side" type recreation vehicles may find it beyond their capability. The last climb, just before Clover, is steep and probably dangerous for unskilled drivers.

(3-B) Return to the Nile from Clover Springs through Mud Springs

The downhill direction, back to Mud Springs is a good route to return on, if you are hiking. The western views along this trail are outstanding for almost 6 miles to the south. This route eventually connects back to forest roads near Mud Springs. Through much of its length this trail traverses the ridge just outside Wilderness. Please do not drive vehicles off the established route to the west to help the Forest Service protect Wilderness value. The chapter on Little Bald #5 has a companion description of the Mud Springs route.

(4) Hiking in from Goose Prairie on the Nile Ridge Wilderness Trail #974. Don't mistake this for the Goose Prairie Trail #972 taking you the opposite direction to the top of American Ridge, see American Ridge Lookout #7. The trailhead is now a mile to the west of Goose Prairie but the old timers simply crossed the Bumping River near the Goose Prairie store at a natural ford.

ADDITIONAL VIEWING OPPORTUNITIES when traveling to Clover Springs and Little Bald Lookout include:

- **Saddle Camp Trailhead, Halfway Flats Trail #961:** One possible side trip is the hike along the Little Bald Trail stretching between Saddle Camp Trailhead and Halfway Flats. This single tread trail winds back down to Halfway Flats through interesting and unique rock talus areas. It is suitable for hikers but mountain bikers also favor it as there are any number of opportunities to break a leg, skin your knees, or just bleed. The views from this trail are outstanding and unique. If you travel this trail, take water and enough provision for a day.

- **Hike to Flat Iron Lake or drop on to the Bumping River.** This trailhead, off Forest Road #1600 between Little Bald Lookout #5 and Clover Springs #18 is the beginning of Trail #957. Flat Iron Lake was once the setting of a cabin or two, probably associated with unpatented mineral claims. Trail # 957 drops to the bottom at the Soda Springs Bridge, Soda Springs Campground, and a **CCC Campground Shelter**. **Soda Springs**, located on the south side of the river, not to be mistaken for Soda Springs Campground near Kloochman Rock in the Tieton Basin. That spring was once a well known landmark, made famous by The William o. Douglas book, *"Of Men and Mountains"*.

SEE ALSO

- *Road Trips,* Handout, available at the Naches Ranger Station.
- A topographic map is essential for exploring this area or accessing Edgar Rock Lookout #3.
- Little Bald Lookout #5 and the many interesting features related to this landmark.
- Gossett, Gretta: *Beyond the Bend* for Local history and lore.
- Spring Ira, *Lookouts*, for reference to Clover Springs, p. 201.

19

Mt. Aix Lookout Site

7,766 - 7772 Feet Elevation

T15N, R13E, Section 18

Remote site in the heart of William O. Douglas Wilderness

- ACCESS AT A GLANCE:

Two challenging Wilderness trail hiking routes from remote trailheads in either the Bumping Basin near Copper Creek or the Rattlesnake Basin from near McDaniel Lake.

- **Lookout Style/Year:** Started as a cabin in the 1920s
    Early Cupola cabin 1923 – 1951 (less possibly 1961).
- **Facilities Present:** Land shapes and much cable and wire.
- **Near by Lookouts and Observation Sites:** Mt Aix is relatively isolated, but Bismarck Peak
    can be visited from these routes if you have calculated your time of return.
- **Fire Lookout Panorama Photo date**: 1929.
- **Difficulty getting to the lookout site** on a scale of 1 (easy) to 5 (difficult): **4**
- **Once there, difficulty to find the actual lookout remains** on a scale of 1 (easy) to 5 (difficult): **1**

Mt. Aix is the highest peak in the William O. Douglas Wilderness and the old lookout was probably the oldest recorded lookout in Yakima County. Mt. Aix peak is remote, the upper slopes are above timberline and rugged. Access is over the Mt. Aix Trail either from McDaniel Trailhead in the Rattlesnake Northfork Drainage or from the Deep Creek Road west of Bumping Lake.

The Mt. Aix Lookout house was constructed in 1923 and could have been repaired or reconstructed at a later date. It was destroyed in 1951 (USDA records). This lookout station was originally used because the location is central to the Mt. Aix country where domestic sheep abounded, but the remote location proved to be a logistic problem and the lookout was abandoned early in the lookout era. Little information on the station and outbuildings remains. The peak is a small earthen platform which must have been associated with a smaller adjacent structure on the steep east side approximately 30 yards below the peak, probably an old storage building or it could have served as housing, or just shelter from the wind. Water would have to be brought from some distance but snow probably filled the gap in early summer. The lookout was serviced through "Lookout Camp" at the head of Dog Creek along Trail #982. Portions of the old telephone line extending from Dog Creek remain.

Some records remain to suggest that Aix was the only Lookout on the Naches District until 1931 when two others were constructed. By 1935 there were eight lookouts completed for a total value of $4,569.49. Camping on Mt. Aix is possible if you are willing to wedge yourself into the small flat spot on the east side of the peak. However, be warned that winds pick up in the evening at this elevation, throughout the summer and fall. I recommend camping at lower, protected elevations, thus "Lookout Camp". I have been told that Mt. Aix was abandoned because of the number of "off" days when it was in the clouds, or as they say, "socked in". I presume the constant and high winds, as well as the remote location also doomed the lookout. I was a wilderness ranger on the Naches for 17 years and a late August "camp out" on Aix was the only time I ever had to abandon a camp, stuff my ballooning tent into a pack and flee back to lower, more protected location.

SETTING

The Mt. Aix Lookout peered to the West into the North Fork of Rattlesnake Creek, one of the most remote spots in the William O. Douglas Wilderness. There, in late summer, 1896 a local sheep herder, perished with over 1,122 sheep under unusual circumstances. The story is told in Gossett local history, in **Jack Nelson's** entertaining book *We Never Got Away*, and in my Yakima Herald article in 1996. Unable to illustrate without waving my arms, let it be said that, when put together, the myth never fails to live up to its potential as a true "old western tale of life and death in the mountains". **Hindoo John** will remain one of the most fascinating and colorful of the old time shepherdess and his story is as mysterious as it is interesting. See "Clover Springs #18 for the further discussion of Hindoo John and his tragic demise.

Reflection on Hindoo John's predicament: On August 28, 1996 I camped on the peak of Mt. Aix in an effort to learn more, first hand, about the untimely demise of Hindoo John, almost exactly one hundred years or so before. Everything was going fine at my little camp on Mt. Aix until around 6pm when the winds started picking up and eventually ran me back into my small pup tent, which was quickly changing from a tent into a kite. Eventually, I feared for my life, wadded my tent into my pack, and fled back toward the Bumping down a switch back or two to re-established a hasty camp in a flat spot even smaller then the one I had just fled, thankfully sheltered by the ridge and trees. In the morning, a small group of hikers stumbled over my camp at around 6am, no doubt trying to beat the rush in the long day hike (48 switchbacks!) to Aix. Their muttering about such the poor location for a camp went unanswered: I pitied them for their ignorance and said nothing. But I did learn one thing:

Whatever the hazard to which John succumbed, the mountains are full of surprises, and not all of them friendly. If you hike in this area carry the ten essentials, walk softly, and be ready to flee if need be, even if it doesn't rhyme. A Mountain itinerary is really just a suggestion, drafted in the warmth of the home fire, and there are no contracts with the higher spirits dictating that it must or even can be followed once you start up the trail. In fact, it is better to operate within option B until the need for Option C is mandated.

Large Mt Hemlock, once listed on the National Register of Big trees, is located in the head of Little Hindoo Basin. Getting to this tree takes 9 hours of hiking, the short way via Road #1500 Trailheads. From the top of Aix you get a pretty darn poor view of the tree, some 3 miles to the southwest. Well, Actually, you get a pretty darn poor view of the grove it oversees as it thrives in a thicket of young trees near a small meadow and the unnamed boat shaped basalt dyke that is as mysterious and imposing as it's tree neighbor, as it should be, for effect. **DISCLAIMER**: As this book goes to press it has NOT been determined if the once Champion Mt. Hemlock survived the Schneider Springs Fire of 2021. I promise to have that correction clearly listed in the 14th or 15th edition of this book.

Meeks Table: T15N, R14E, Section 5, McDaniel Lake Road #1502 to Meeks Table, turnoff spur #1502 – 610: Park at the trailhead and walk in two miles to the western spine of the table where an old game trail awaits you, unsigned. Occasionally local hikers may place sticks, rocks, or bits of clothing to suggest, possibly, the way up. Meeks Table is a Research Natural Area, chosen because domestic livestock have never grazed on this exclusive basalt table. Noted for its old growth, pinegrass environment, it is also unique for its outstanding views and ancient, gnarled ponderosa snags. CAUTION: the only way up is the only way down in a practical sort of way.

GETTING THERE

- (1) FROM Deep Creek Road #1808 to the trailhead for the #982 Trail.

- (2) OR FROM McAix Trailhead Near McDaniel Lake,
  - Trail #982 near the end of Road #1502
  - OR where ever the road ends at the time.

NOTE: Forest Road #1502 may be closed on alternate years due to the Rattlesnake Bridge washout.

(1) From Deep Creek Road: motor past Bumping Lake Campground on Road #1800 and proceed west to the junction of the Swamp Lake Trailhead turnoff. Stay left and head up Deep Creek on road #1808 to the Copper Creek Bridge where trail #982 departs to the south. You will find good parking here and dispersed camping is available close to the creek. 4,000 feet of climbing over multiple switchbacks and a six mile stretch of trail awaits you with open arms.

(2) From the North Fork of the Rattlesnake, McDaniel Lake Trailhead: The end of the road McAix Trailhead offers plenty of camping and parking. Expect hunters during deer and elk seasons. From here you will head west over Dog Creek and into the Hindoo Basin on Trail #982. Lookout Camp, about half way to the lookout offers water, shelter, and views. Stay on the Mt. Aix Trail #982 and proceed to the lookout for a 3,000 foot gain over 12 miles. Round trip hiking this way is not practical when you throw in driving to and from.

SEE ALSO

- Hiler, Mike: *Mt Aix, a Historical Perspective*, Signpost Magazine, March 1989
- Cyr, Suzy, Tanum, the Story of Bumping Lake (great story of this area) 2022
- Gossett, Gretta: See Mt. Aix discussion, p. 476-477
- Hiler, Mike: *The Hindoo John Story*, Yakima Herald, 12-24-1998 p.3C or, Forest Service Lookout edition, 1997

- Google "**Kennith Arnold**, June 16, 1947" for local history: Most accounts of Arnold wrongly indicate the location of his sighted nine undulating silver discs was near Mt Rainier instead of the actual location over Mt. Aix. Quite simply everyone knows where Mt. Rainier is, almost no one knows where Mt. Aix is, Thankfully, AND, why did they really move out of Mt Aix Lookout in 1951, at the height of the Lookout era.

- Hindoo Herder Report: *in Wenatchee Historical overview, page 7.3, apparently taken from the E. J. Fenby Management Plan, 1933 Grazing Atlas reports housed in the depths of the Yakima Valley Museum. It begins* "in 1896 a band of some 3,500 head of sheep, belonging to Sam Cameron was being run on a creek now known as Hindoo Creek, in charge of a Hindoo herder......" (caution: primary references on the specifics of the Hindoo Story do vary).

20

Tumac Mountain Lookout Site

6,304 Feet Elevation

T14N, R12E, Section 8 near south border

GPS Coordinates: N46d -- 42.734m, W121d -- 21.182m

William O. Douglas Wilderness north of White Pass on the Cascade Crest

Lookout site may be partially in Lewis County

- ACCESS AT A GLANCE:

Several different Wilderness trail approaches off Highway 12 near White Pass
or from Twin Sisters Lakes, via Bumping Lake Road, with some hiking thrown in.
- **Lookout Style/Year:** Older style Lookout 1920s – 1960s.
- **Facilities Present:** Concrete foundation pads, great view of Mosquito Valley.
- **Fire Lookout Panorama Photo date:** 1929.
- **Nearby Lookout and Observation Sites**: Spiral Butte Observation Site.
- **Difficulty getting to the lookout site** on a scale of 1 (easy) to 5 (difficult): **4**
- **Once there, difficulty to find the actual lookout remains** on a scale of 1 (easy) to 5 (difficult): **1**

Tumac Mountain was named by Albert H. Sylvester, an early forester, in memory of **two** Scotch sheepherders named

McDuff and McAdam, who earlier raced their bands of sheep to get to the higher pasture first each season somewhere before1904. The lookout was constructed in the 1920's, though it was probably managed by the Packwood District (now the Cowlitz Valley District) out of the Gifford Pinchot Forest most of the time. Owing to the open peak view on Tumac Mountain, as well as the exposed condition here, it is probable that this station sat on the ground.

This station was the contact point between the Tieton, Naches and Packwood Ranger Districts (indicated by different trail number prefixes) and is also a contact point for Lewis and Yakima County forest fire suppression efforts. A flat spot on top of a peak and at the junction of several counties and Ranger Districts, not to mention National Forests, it would be impossible to determine which county could claim the Lookout, a true "no man's land". In any case, the old 1929 panorama photo of Tumac will give about as much information as anything about what was actually happening on the lookout in the early days.

Former Lookouts at this unique cinder-cone mountaintop include Bob Baldwin (1950) and Lloyd Raft (1963?). Bob remembered taking a bus from Spokane to his new job out of Packwood and the bus driver setting him off at Cayuse Pass to negotiate the rest of the trip on his own, suitcase in hand.

SETTING

Once described as a post glacial cinder-cone, this unique mountain, north of White Pass and accessible from the Pacific Crest Trail is certainly something special in the in the category of cinder cones. There is apparently some question about its "post glacial" claim, but it seems logical that the last glaciers would have heavily carved this soft red, pumice landform had the two been in contact. Tumac is surrounded by a variegated landscape of short flowing basalt ridges and numerous mosquito infested ponds which make up the surrounding Tumac Plateau, also called **"Mosquito Valley"**.

Now a unique observation site Tumac Mountain offers great views into Twin Sisters Lakes and Indian Creek Meadows (Mosquito Valley), as well as Tieton Basin and north and south over the Pacific Crest Trail. The unique east and west views offer outstanding sunrise and sunsets as well as eyeball to eyeball views of Mt. Rainier and (to a lesser extent) Mt. Adams.

Either Mark Hitchcock or Ralph Hagaroud (I can't remember which, perhaps both), former Wilderness Rangers in this area once submitted an annual Wilderness/ back country Patrol Report that predicted an eventual eruption of Tumac but it has yet to occur. However, when it does happen, we will have Mark and Ralph to thank for their timely notice!

The John McAllister demise, near **Indian Creek Falls**. John McAllister does not relate directly to Tumac Mountain Lookout, or any other lookout but the story of his demise near Indian Creek Falls is certainly memorable, as well as a monument to the rugged miners who wandered all over these hills around 1900.

In the fall of 1912 John was returning from his "Black Jack Mine" (See Miners Ridge Lookout, #6) to his cabin in what is now the bottom of Rimrock Lake. At the time this was known as the Bootjack Country, due to the nearness of the pioneer landmark, **Book Jack Rock**. Failing to show up at his cabin, foul play was suspected but winter was on and the Earth continued to turn.

Late the next spring two boys, fishing Indian Creek explored above the falls and stumbled across John's remains at the most desirable place to pass away that can be imagined. Sometime later someone carved on the tree that he was (hopefully) propped up against and his remains were returned, hopefully as well, to a graveyard somewhere with the rest of the local pioneers, fittingly or just buried nearby as no plastic bags then existed. DISCLAIMER #3: A tree marking the spot of John's demise has recently fallen and the carved headstone obscured so if you wish to find it, it probably isn't there.

GETTING THERE

- FROM (1) Highway 12 at White Pass: Trail #44
  - by way of Pacific Crest Trail #2000.
- OR (2) FROM Dog Lake to the PCT over Trail #1106.
- OR (3) FROM Highway 410 by way of Goose Prairie and Bumping Lake
  - over Trail #980 at Deep Creek Trailhead (Forest Road #1808),

  And on from Twin Sisters Lakes to Trail #944 to the top of Tumac Mountain.

There are several access routes for Tumac Mountain the preferred being the day-hike along the Pacific Crest Trail north of White Pass. The route from Dog Lake by way of Cramer Lake is purported to be easier but for some reason not as popular. Some visitors come in from Twin Sisters Lakes though that primitive route alone adds several rugged hours of driving to the trailhead. Overnight camping to access the peak is a great idea for those who prefer a more leisurely visit and primitive William O. Douglas Wilderness camping abounds near the Trail #144 junction.

(1) From the White Pass Pacific Crest Trail #2000 South Trailhead:

Access to Tumac Mountain is probably best by leaving White Pass, traveling north along the Pacific Crest Trail #2000, and departing east along Trail #44. The climb to the Tumac Peak is steep but the views are rewarding. The downside of this route is that you have to climb, and then drop back to Tumac Plateau, meaning you will have some uphill on the return, PCT route.

(2) From Dog Lake, off Highway 12 two miles east of White Pass: A similar route, and shorter than the White Pass route above, I am told by 1951 lookout Bob Baldwin. This is almost the same route as (1) above except leaving from Dog Lake, climbing to Cramer Lake, traversing to Dumbbell Lake, and from there attaching yourself to the PCT which you will follow to the Tumac Trail #44.

(3) From Twin Sisters Lakes, by way of Highway 410 and on to the Bumping Lake paved road. To simplify these instructions, flip to the "Getting there" for Miner's Ridge #6 in this book and follow the alternate route to Deep Creek Trailhead:

From Deep Creek Trailhead: Hike up to Twin Sisters Lakes, and onto the northeast end of the #44 Tumac Trail. From there you have the climb that is required by all routes, as Tumac Peak stands above the Tumac Plateau from all sides as cinder cones do, similar to the fact that we seldom make conscious decisions on the proper end of an ice cream cone to eat first or, "Its better to work out from the known than inward from the unknown".

SEE ALSO

- Abbott, A: *"The Geology of the Northwest portion of the Mt. Aix Quadrangle,*

  Washington, 1953. University Microfilms, Ann Arbor, Michigan.

- Directions to Miners Ridge Lookout #6 this book for Deep Creek Trailhead directions.

- Gossett, Gretta: Tumac Mountain, p. 487

- Hiler, Mike, *Mystery Pioneer John McAllister,* Yakima Herald 12-10-1998, p.3C

Norse Peak Wilderness and Pierce County Area Lookouts

21. Arch Rock Trail Shelter site and proposed Lookout, Pierce County

22. Crystal Peak Lookout Site: Mt. Rainier Park, Pierce County

23. Norse Peak Lookout Site, North Bend Ranger District, Pierce Co.

Because the area around Chinook Pass is associated with the Naches District, just as it isn't, these three sites are lumped together. They are accessed generally from north of Chinook Pass and south of Pyramid Pass but they are mostly outside Yakima County, at least technically. If you plan your trip accordingly, you may be able to visit a couple of these sites on a given day, though Arch Rock, not a real lookout, is closer to Government Meadows and is best visited in conjunction with your visit to Raven Roost Lookout #7.

ROUND MOUNTAIN
LOOKOUT

SNOQUALMIE N.F.
ELEV. 5971

— Emily Watkins

E. BROWN

21

Arch Rock Panorama Photo Lookout Site and Arch Rock historic Trail Shelter Site

Neither of which exist today

5,493 Feet Elevation

T18N, R11E, Section 22

1934 Panorama overlook and associated trail shelter site

No lookout structure was placed at this site.

Norse Peak Wilderness near the Pacific Crest Trail

Pierce County Washington

- ACCESS AT A GLANCE:

By way of Pacific Crest Trail from several optional trailheads north of Chinook Pass
or from Raven Roost, lookout #7, this book.
- **Lookout Style and Year:** Panorama photo point, trail shelter, no Lookout building.
- **Facilities Present:** No lookout station, an old trail shelter once stood ½ mile east of the viewpoint.
- **Nearby Lookout and Observation Sites:** Raven Roost Lookout #7.
- **Fire Lookout Panorama Photo date**: 1934, this unique panorama photo to be seen

in the Naches Ranger Station visitors conference room.

- Difficulty getting to the lookout site on a scale of 1 (easy) to 5 (difficult): **4**

- Once there, difficulty to find the actual lookout remains on a scale of 1 (easy) to 5 (difficult): **6**

Arch Rock is located in the north of the Norse Peak Wilderness just west of the **Pacific Crest Trail**. It is near the site of an old trail shelter, now long since disappeared and managed in its invisible state by the Snoqualmie Ranger District, Enumclaw. There is no indication that an actual lookout was placed at or near Arch Rock and no records I can locate directly indicate the lookout was actually built though the 1934 panorama photo from the site indicates it was considered.

That interesting lookout panorama photograph from "Arch Rock, August 16, 1934" is hanging in the Naches Ranger District Visitor Conference room. The panorama was taken from the ground and not atop a lookout building confirming the "no Lookout at Arch Rock" theory. No doubt the panorama photo at Arch Rock was taken during the planning phase and no lookout was ever built for whatever reason was good enough at the time. The amazing point of the panorama photo (facing 120 Degrees), however, is the camera pack boxes that transported the photographic panorama equipment from lookout to lookout by pack string.

Arch rock is a typical example of the lookout sites that were studied but not utilized. Viewing the 1934 panorama shows that it had some potential, but not enough to justify placing a lookout station. If YOU can find an old foundations or a **bench mark** (see Introduction) close to the location on the map, the credit will go out to you as the actual discoverer of one of the most mysterious lookouts in the Cascades!

SETTING

At one time **Trail Shelters** dotted the backcountry landscape. Today only the old Adirondack Shelter at Long Lake remains. You can see the Long Lake Shelter when you hike to Jumpoff Lookout #4 by way of **Louie Gap.** There you can study the unique design of the classis Adirondack and wonder that this shelter seems to have survived from the 1930s in relatively original condition. A bit of maintenance over the years, no doubt, has a lot to do with the longevity of the Long Lake Shelter, or perhaps the swarms of mosquitoes have propped it up with their sheer numbers.

GETTING THERE

- (1) FROM Government Meadows: South on PCT Trail #2000.

- (2) OR FROM Road #1917 trailhead for Louisiana Saddle Trail #945A.

- (3) OR from Raven Roost by way of Road #1902, Lookout site #17

    - on Trail #951 to PCT Trail #2000

    - and on North three miles to the site of the old trail shelter.

Arch Rock is best approached from Crow Creek. Progress to Raven Roost (see Lookout #17) and take the trail west out from Raven Roost to Cougar Valley, turn to the right on trail #951 to the PCT (2 ½ miles) and walk north a couple of miles to the junction of the PCT and Arch Rock User Trail. The old shelter site is up this trail 50 yards and you can journey further up the cliffs for great views to the west.

(1) From Government Meadows, south on PCT #2000: Depart from the PCT Pyramid Pass Trailhead south toward Government Meadows. The instructions for this trailhead are exhaustive in the

Pyramid Peak Lookout #13 section in this book. You will hike a couple miles south to Government Meadows where you will cross the old wagon road, now active 4x4 trail. Hike on south past Louisiana Saddle using a map and locate the Arch rock camping area near a cryptic trail junction. Hike off the trail to the west in a large area that has hosted many camps over the years, to a cliffy area where the lookout must have been planned, before it was unplanned. The trail shelter location is up for interpretation, but it appears to be just west of this trail junction and camping area. Well, at least it's a good camping area and not a bad place to spend a night.

(2) From Road #1917 Trailhead for Louisiana Saddle on Trail #945A to the PCT: Hike west to the PCT and then follow the directions above to help you find the location of the former Shelter and/or the lookout.

(3) From Raven Roost Lookout #7, by way of Road #1900 to #1902, 13 miles to

> Trail # 951, hiking on through Cougar Valley to the Pacific Crest Trail #2000 and then

> several miles north to an old Arch Rock Shelter site and camping spot near a trail junction.

NOTE

A **1937 Snoqualmie National Forest map** legend lists (1) Permanent Lookout Stations, (2) Emergency Lookout Observation Points, (3) Patrol Lookout Point, and (4) Triangulation Station (site of a benchmark). Triangulation stations were easily visible landmarks used by lookouts to practice their "Osborne" fire finder skills which helps to more accurately locate fires. Photo panoramas usually indicate lookouts but not always. Arch Rock was probably a lookout patrol point much like Lookout Camp (#19 this book).

SEE ALSO

- Historic Documents: Mt. Baker-Snoqualmie National Forest trail shelter overview.

22

Crystal Peak Lookout Site

6,595 feet elevation

Most likely T17N, R10E, Section 34 or possibly
T16N, R10E, Section 2

Pierce County

North of Chinook Pass, Several hundred feet west of Yakima County

Mt. Rainier National Park

- ACCESS AT A GLANCE:

Climbing Crystal Lake Trail off Highway 410 from near
and North of the Sunrise Mt Rainier Park entrance within
Mt. Rainier National Park.

- Lookout style and Year: Older style Lookout 1934 to 1950s
(some say late 60s?).
- Facilities Present: Concrete Footing blocks with protruding
anchor pins.
- Nearby Lookouts and Observation Points: Norse Peak Lookout
#21 this book, the view down
into the Naches Basin from the Chinook Pass Overlook, and
trail views hiking
the Pacific Crest Trail North or South from Chinook Pass.
- No Panorama Photo on record
- Difficulty getting to the lookout site on a scale of 1 (easy) to 5
(difficult): **3 or 4**

- Once there, difficulty to find the actual lookout remains on a scale of 1 (easy) to 5 (difficult)**: 3**

Although Crystal Lake Lookout is outside of Yakima County and is accessed almost exclusively from Pierce County. I include it here because it is a great day hike side-trip when you are visiting Chinook Pass or Crystal Mt Ski Area. It all gets sort of confusing up at Crystal Lake as this lookout is described as Crystal Peak Lookout, Crystal Lake Lookout, Crystal Point Lookout, Crystal Peak and Crystal Lookout, and, owing to the steep trail, probably a few other choice names. This area is prone to cross country travel, owing to the open, alpine topography, and is NOT prone to cross country travel owing to some impassible cliffs around the old lookout peak site.

Crystal Peak Lookout was one of 8 lookouts that once made up the Mt. Rainier lookout system. It was apparently similar to and built in connection with the Tolmie, Freemont and Gobblers Knob Lookouts by a Seattle Company. The style was an older design two story with a ground floor level storage room, probably for storing cases of pork and beans.

As related by Gene Casey, Park Ranger, (1962 – 1998) the already weakened lookout was badly damaged by snow around 1972 or 73. In 1974 Jim Wintworth a park road worker attempted to finish off the suffering with 34 sticks of dynamite, which apparently created more noise than damage, but in any case the lookout is now just a memory.

SETTING

Chinook Pass was punched west up **Normile Grade** from the mouth of Morse Creek and over the top near Tipsoo Lake in 1931. The new pass was dedicated by serving of Peaches from the Yakima Valley topped by cream from the west side diaries. The Normile Grade construction camp became the Timber Creek Summer homes, Larry Taylor's cabin was located just below the present Morse Creek bridge and Clarence Truitt's Cabin is located up Morse Creek a couple of unpredictable miles on a predictably rutted and washed out road. The old Morgan prospecting cabin is further up the creek. The Hidden Treasure mineshaft is still generally open on the spur road that departs southwest from the Chinook Pass chain up area (winter gate) west of the Morse Creek Bridge.

GETTING THERE

- (1) FROM Highway 410 at Chinook Pass PCT Trailhead North

    - BY WAY OF Pacific Crest #20000 Trail north to Crystal Lake and beyond.

- (2) OR FROM highway 410 near Sunrise Road turnoff by way of the Crystal Lake Trail.

(1) Chinook Pass Highway is the State Route 410 Cascades Mountain Pass between Naches, WA, and Greenwater, often known as the Stephen F. Mather Parkway. It alone should be a whole chapter in this book because more visitors have visited the Chinook Pass Highway viewpoint than all the other lookouts combined in this book. The Chinook Pass vista is located across the highway from the Chinook Pass Pacific Crest Trail Trailhead and the vista-view is down and into a classic glacial basin to the east which is remarkable, outstanding, spectacular and just damn OK. The view from and into Lake Tipsoo, a mile to the west (on the Pierce County side) is also memorable. There is a local legend that no one ever passed Tipsoo Lake without taking a photo of it, making it the most viewed lake in the world. Those without cameras don't really exist.

(2) OR by way of the Crystal Lake trailhead off Highway 410, 5 miles south of the Rainier Park boundary or a mile or so north of the Sunrise Turnoff. Driving east from Greenwater, or west from Chinook Pass you will notice the entrance road to the Crystal Mt. Ski Area several miles north of the Crystal Lake Trailhead. The Crystal Lake Trailhead, on Highway 410 is not usually signed, but you will see cars parked on both sides of Highway 410, or at least plenty of parking opportunity on both sides of the highway. The popular Trail departs to the East. The trail climbs about one mile and branches off to the left to Crystal Lake. Stay right, then expect more climbing up to the old lookout site. Because of the cliffs in this area, the Crystal Lakes and the Crystal Lookout are close but accessibility between the two is difficult.

SEE ALSO

- Norse Peak Lookout #23

23

Norse Peak Lookout Site

6,856 Feet Elevation

T17N, R11E, near Section line between sections 17 and 18

Norse Peak Wilderness

Managed By Snoqualmie Ranger District,

Enumclaw Station, Mt. Baker/Snoqualmie National Forest

Pierce County, a hop, skip, and jump to Yakima County

Norse Peak Wilderness namesake, overlooks Crystal Mt. Ski Area

- ACCESS AT A GLANCE:

North of Chinook Pass, just off Pacific Crest Trail # 2000
near Basin Lake or access trail
off the Crystal Mountain Ski Area Road.

- Lookout Style and Year: Older style not well known, possibly
1930? – 1956?

- Facilities Present: Not much.

- Fire Lookout Panorama Photo date: 1929.

- Nearby Lookouts and Observation Points: Crystal Peak
Lookout #23

Raven Roost #7, Pyramid Peak #13.

- Difficulty getting to the lookout site on a scale of 1 (easy) to 5
(difficult): **3**

- Once there, difficulty to find the actual lookout remains on a
scale of 1 (easy) to 5 (difficult): **3**

Norse Peak is the namesake of Norse Peak Wilderness, probably one of the few Wilderness areas for which legislators couldn't find an expired reprobate or cuddly animal suitable for the appropriate moniker. This mountaintop looks to the west into the Crystal Basin wherein resides the Crystal Mountain Ski Resort, to the west into Lake Basin, and to the northeast into Big Crow Basin. I refrain from mentioning that there is a possibility that half of Norse Peak Lookout site isn't actually in Norse Peak Wilderness or that "Fife Peak Wilderness" or "Crow Basin Wilderness" would have been a far better names for that small, but stunning Wilderness.

The Norse Peak Lookout station was probably placed around 1931 and removed in 1956. The Jess Rose notes suggest a camp here before 1931. Ira Spring shows no record of this lookout site and no station remains on this peak. Norse Peak was technically on the White River Ranger District before consolidation, now the Snoqualmie District, managed out of Enumclaw in Pierce County.

Former Lookouts at Norse Peak include Dora Hunt and Maxine Ilipkoe who worked the lookout together in 1944. They had to learn lookout skills and pass some sort of proficiency test before occupying their station. Skills typically taught to lookouts include map reading, weather reporting, the use of fire-finding instruments, elementary fire-fighting, and window washing. Lookouts were also issued a "Fire Pack" which was kept at the duty station and included fire gear and, in my case, a cross cut saw lashed over the top of the pack in a horseshoe.

SETTING

Namesake of Norse Peak Wilderness, a good view but not remarkable in contrast to the area: Someone must have been Norwegian. Workers who constructed the old lookout had to negotiate a rugged three mile access trail. It is reported that on "July 11, their little lookout was rocked by an icy mountain-top blizzard." Although infrequent, short, passing storms of snow, sleet, or hail could be expected any month of the summer at all the lookouts in this collection.

GETTING THERE

- : - (1) FROM Highway 410 south of Silver Springs turning off toward Crystal Mt Ski Area
    - on (Gold Hill?) Road #1930 and taking Trail #1191 to the East (or is it Road #7176
    - and Trail #1161?) four or five miles up the road toward the ski area.
- (2) OR From Pacific Crest Trail #2000 near Lake Basin: ½ mile cross country
    - by way of Scout Pass.
- (3) OR hiking out of Morse Creek area on the Berar Gap Trail up to the Pacific Crest Trail
    - and progressing north to the head of Big Crow Basin and on up to Norse Peak.

Before you start looking for the Norse Peak Trail you need to know that there are NO two maps of the Crystal Mountain Basin that agree on trail name, number, location, trailhead location, road name, etc. Therefore, any trail or road name or number I give will confuse you half the time, and if there are two of you, all the time. However, I hope the following directions, followed judiciously, will get you there with as little "lostness" as possible 100% of the time, and at the end of the day, lost or found, from anywhere in the Crystal Basin, you will be able to find your way home by simply going downhill toward either Spokane or Seattle.

(1) The best way to hike to Norse Peak Lookout site is to start from the trail which departs the Crystal Mountain Ski Area access Road #7190 or on some maps and some signing Road #7166, four or

five miles after turning off Highway 410 near Silver Springs and possibly 34 miles or so from Enumclaw. The trailhead departs the east side of the road, with parking on the left, and is fortunately hard to find, as no clear signing exists, or if it exists the trail is identified as the #1161 Goat Lake Trail or the #1191 Norse Peak Trail. I suggest driving to the Ski Area, ask a few questions, turn around and slowly drive back, looking closely on the right side of the road for something that might vaguely look like a trailhead. The Goat Lake Trail #1161 which may interest you, for example is very near the beginning of stub-road #7176 although some maps indicate this road should be # 7175, or is it road #7190-410. We may never know. Ahhh, the glorious hours spent trying to find a semi-nonexistent trailhead when all maps disagree, and reality suggests you are not going to find it anyway! Anyway, when you finally find the trail, park on the east side of the road, giving thanks to the Trailhead Gods, and start up the trail as if you really knew where you are going. Reading the Description #2 below may also help some.

(2) Hiking on the PCT between Chinook Pass and Government Meadow you will drop into the Crow Creek Basin to the east, with lots of high open alpine basins, the kind that sheepherders loved or perhaps created with a match. Crow Basin, Big Crow Basin, and Basin Lake, are all attractive and unique land features that typify the area. Airplane meadows and other less known but romantic features abound here. As you progress along the crest, west of Crow Basin you will reach a point, near Basin Lake here it would be a shame not to scamper up to the top of this mysteriously named and unmemorable Norse Peak, once defined by a now nonexistent lookout but then, isn't that what the past is all about?

(3) Another Departure point for the PCT access route in this area is the Bear Gap Trailhead in the Morse Creek Basin: This route is a bit longer than the access route from Crystal Ski area, but it gives you more PCT miles, always a plus to those who love to gather PCT miles and abhor zeros. Enter Morse Creek near the Chinook Pass

(Highway 410) chain up area, 5 miles east of Chinook Pass. The Morse Creek Road can be more like a 4x4 trail at times, don't expect it to be an actual forest gravel road suitable for passenger cars. At the Bear Gap Trailhead, near the old Truitt Cabin, you will park and progress up the hill generally north toward the PCT, somewhere up above in the vicinity of Fog City, population 0. From here, progress north on the PCT to the upper Crow Basin, by way of Crown Point, Cement Basin, Scout Pass, and on to Norse Peak near and above Basin Lake. Norse Peak is easy to identify from Basin Lake, up and to the west. Find a good line for alpine bushwhacking and head for the peak or find the mythical trail off the north side.

SEE ALSO

- The PCT north of Chinook Pass is one of the most remarkable alpine areas

    of the entire 2,642 miles between Mexico and Canada.

- My PCT cap, purchased along the trail for reference to above mileage

- Gossett, Gretta: Norse Peak, p. 478

Additional Observation Site
to Consider

TIMBERWOLF
MTN
LOOKOUT
SNOQUALMIE N.F.

E. BROWN

24

Spiral Butte Proposed Lookout Site and Overlook

5,900 - 5920 Feet Elevation

T14N, R12E, Section 32

William O. Douglas Wilderness, East of Dog Lake near White Pass

- ACCESS AT A GLANCE:

Wilderness Trail access off Highway 12 near Clear Lake or from near White Pass
through the Wilderness trail system to challenging, faint, non-system, unmaintained, unsigned
and nearly forgotten Spiral Butte Forest Service Trail.

- Lookout Style/Year: Ira Spring, in his interesting *Lookouts* book lists this as a site
where a trail was built to service the yet un-built lookout, and where no station
was placed. Spiral Butte was known as "Big Peak" before White Pass highway
was constructed over the Cascade Crest in 1951.

- Facilities Present: None were ever placed.

- Nearby Lookout and Observation Sites: Tumac Mountain Lookout Site #20
Round Mt Lookout site #16.

- No known Photographic Panorama

- Difficulty getting to the lookout site on a scale of 1 (easy) to 5 (difficult): **4**

- Once there, difficulty to find the actual lookout remains on a scale of 1 (easy) to 5 (difficult)**: 5**

I added Spiral Butte to my lookout list because some effort was made by the Forest Service to install a lookout there indicating a unique view. Ira Spring, in his book *Lookouts* lists this as a site where a trail was built for a planned lookout but no station was ever placed. If Spiral Butte is good enough for Ira, it's good enough for me. Without the lookout, the trail would have had no practical use, if viewing is considered a practical endeavor. Now it is practically a lost trail.

Before the construction of **White Pass highway**, this peak was well named "**Big Peak**". However, viewed from the air, or from an aerial photo there is no mystery why the Spiral Butte name was changed. From overhead it presents a spiraling lava flow that is unmistakable, though not so apparent without aerial photography. By 1951, the year White Pass Highway was cut over the Cascades, aerial photos were more common and this distinguishing feature probably seemed more descriptive of this large Peak, visible to eastward travelers on the White Pass Highway east of White Pass. This Massive spiraling stone feature falls to Dog Lake to the West and is probably part of the old andesite cinder-cone feature typical of the whole Tumac Plateau. The view on Spiral Butte is stunning, the hike is rigorous, and it just seems fitting to include it here, not so much that it never hosted a lookout but because it never did.

SETTING

Planned lookouts that were never constructed are relatively common. I suppose this is a result of the changing times catching up with new ideas. Suitable access and remoteness, the length of the phone line that had to be maintained, good surrounding visual coverage, along with the availability of water were just a few of the requirements for a lookout. Good radio communication, safety for the guard, also played a part in determining a mountain peak suitable for the effort required to actually pack in lumber and build a remote building. For example, Blowout Mt, to the north between Pyramid Peak and Quartz Mountain Lookout is another such planned site for a lookout that was never built. Forest Service records suggest that in 1933 around $13.56 was expended on the nonexistent Blowout Lookout, probably incurred for horseshoe nails.

Sand Ridge Trailhead has a bit of local history that ties the area from Twin Sisters Lakes, Rimrock Lake, and the White Pass together. At one time, this was the end of the westward road from Yakima, later Highway 5 and eventually, U.S. Highway 12. At that time the Sand Ridge Trailhead was called the Black Jack Trailhead, honoring John McAllister's Mine.

Early in the century the old John McAllister zinc mine, just below Twin Sisters Lakes (See Miner's Ridge #6 for more on that area) was called the **Black Jack Mine** as Black Jack is a moniker for zinc ore. John's Cabin was in what is now the lower port of the bottom of Rimrock Lake. He often used the Black Jack Trail to get back and forth between cabin and mine (see McAllister Tree discussion with Tumac Mountain Lookout #20). Later this trailhead was called "Maggie's Campground" for Maggie (last name unkown), who established a hunting camp of some fame there in the 50s and 60's. Could she have been the first Trail Angel ?

Today Sand Ridge is a well named ridge that has a eloquent sufficiency of sandy soil, compliments of a pre Mount St Helens (type) ash layer deposit assisted by a fortuitous wind, guessing as an amateur geologist. The May 18, 1980 St. Helens ash fall improved the sandy nature of this ridge and trail, not to everyone's liking. In late August, annually, this trail would better be named, "Dusty Ridge".

When you visit the peak over the now abandoned Spiral Butte Trail you may have to depend, in part, on old trail blazes. These axe scribes on trees along the trail edge were once a common way to identify the trail if it was unmaintained for a few years or if it was obscured by snow. This is a good time to explain what trail blazes are and why they exist:

It is often thought that blazes on trees, along a trail were markers for skiers and snow shoers, but in fact, at one time the Forest Service managed a standard for **blazing trees** along most established forest trails. Generally, most districts used an "i" (a swipe with a dot above or a pre-apple prefix)) but there were variations. Also, before plastic trail ribbon was invented (by the devil), prospectors, trappers, and hunters often used a tree blaze to mark a trail as they probably carried a sharp axe anyway. But today, blazes are a thing of the past and mark the way on only the oldest of trails. The Forest Service may still think they blaze trails as per standards, but few National Forest Trails have been blazed in the past 40 years, mostly because of lack of funding since trail clearing and drainage rightly became the highest trail maintenance objectives. Also, the skill of "setting" a good blaze, a double stroke with a sharp single bit axe has now gone the way of the Dodo bird.

Many interesting facts about lookout stations can be additionally gleaned from the many Lookout web sites and postings on the internet. Also, the Washington Trails magazine, Signpost, has printed too many lookout articles to mention. The National Lookout Museum, in Spokane is both interesting and inspiring. If you find yourself becoming a dry-eyed dye-hard lookout fan, I suggest you join the National Fire Fighting Lookout Association or at least visit their web site.

If challenge is yours for the asking, Spiral Butte stands alone as one of the last "hard to get to" lookout sites because, well, it's hard to get to. Another reason I included spiral Butte here, other than it might have been a lookout, is to offer at least one lookout where visiting represents a Wilderness achievement of note. Actually getting to Desolation Peak Lookout, of Jack Kerouac fame (near Ross Lake on the North Cascades), took Kristin and I four tries but it remains one of our favorite moments to finally stand at the peak and stare out at the unfathomable desolation of undisturbed earthen forests, stretching away to infinity.

GETTING THERE

- (1) **FROM highway 12** at the Sand Ridge Trailhead
- **ON** the Sand Ridge Trail #1104 to the Shellrock Lake Trail #1142.
  - **AND ON** to the abandoned Big Peak Trail #1108
  - for a 3 mile climbing bushwack to the site.
- (2) **OR FROM** Highway 12 at Dog Lake Trailhead
  - OVER the Creamer Lake Trail #1106 and on to Spiral Butte
  - (Big Peak) Trail #1108 by way of other connecting trails.

You can approach the Big Peak Trail from either (1) Sand Ridge Trailhead or (2) from Dog Lake by way of connecting Wilderness trails toward Cramer Lake and beyond. To add to the uncertain name and remote location, the Spiral Butte trail was abandoned some years ago due to lack of interest by local hikers and therefore by the Forest Service, compliments of budget cuts from higher up.

(1) You can approach the Big Peak Trail by following the Sand Ridge Trail #1104 west from the Sand Ridge Trailhead, just off Highway 12, and a couple miles west of Rimrock Lake. A ways up the #1104 Trail you will switch engines to the Shellrock Trail #1142 delivering you to the abandoned Spiral Butte Trail #1108 somewhere around Section 28. As you work your way to the top keep an eye out for the trail blazes defining the way to the peak and near the top be on the lookout for the brass cap USGS benchmark. If you wish to make an

overnight backpack of Spiral Butte peak, the trail in from Dog Lake offers good opportunities for camping a lot of great Wilderness, when the mosquitoes are not out in force after the first annual frost, often in late August.

(2) Dog Lake, adjacent to Highway 410 two miles east of White Pass begins the longer approach to Spiral Butte but for those expecting to backpack or tent camp this route offers the most variety. Hike up the Cramer Lake trail to Cramer Lake, navigate the trail junctions back toward Shellrock Lake and search for the conspicuously unsigned Big Peak trail junction which has been replaced with lack of interest. The trail to the peak is an arduous three mile climb where the lookout that never was welcomes you to the view that always is.

Wilderness camping is available on this trip at Cramer Lake or Shellrock Lake. Please abide by Wilderness regulations and camp back from the lakeshore at least 100 feet, pack out what you bring in , and practice the latest method of dealing with human waste.

SEE ALSO

- Geology of the Mt. Aix Quadrangle, USGS

- Better yet, cross-country hike the ground around Tumac Mountain for a unique Geology course, guided by a good compass or GPS. You can get lost there with little effort.

25

The Rest of the Lookouts in Yakima County

There are 11 more lookout sites in Yakima County but those sites did not coordinate with the Naches Basin (Wenatchee National Forest) fire programs and I know little about them. They are represented by the 8 sites on the Yakama Nation, 2 lookouts on the very western boundary of the County, managed by the Gifford Pinchot Forest, and one additional DNR site generally east and south of Yakima.

The Yakama Nation sites are all administered by the Yakama Nation often on closed land and I am advising to NOT visit these sites unless you have specific permission from the Toppenish Office. The 1934 Metsker map is a good source for locating these sites. They are listed below alphabetically:

25. Goat Butte: T8N, R11E, Section 3

26. Hagerty Butte: T7N, R15E, Section 31

27. Jennie's Butte: T11N, R12E, Section 34

28. Lakeview Mountain: T10N, R11E, Section 2

29. McKays Butte: T8N, R15E, Section 28

30. Panther Creek: T10N, R13E, Section 27

31. Satus Peak: TT9N, R16E, Section 24

32. Signal Peak: T9N, R13E, Section 36

The three final Yakima County sites that had no working relationship with the Naches Basin Lookouts, They include two lookouts on the west side of the Cascades in the vicinity of Mt. Adams, often thought of as more in Skamania County (though technically in Yakima County) and one additional site I want to mention because it is also in Yakima County.

They are:

> 33. Midway Lookout, Gifford Pinchot Forest: T10N, R10E, Section 13

> 34. Mount Adams Lookout, Gifford Pinchot: T8N, R10E, S12

> 35. Sedge Ridge Lookout, DNR: T12N, R15E, Section 29

AND: Bdeeb, bdeeb, bdeeb, that's all folks!!

Lookout Stories

A Day on Watch

Grayback Lookout

By Wendy Warren

Wind was lashing at the windows, pushing with such ferocity I was sure the glass would blow out. I huddled on the floor, pressed against the drawers that formed the base of the bunk. With the wool blanket over my head and tucked securely around me, I wondered if this was much protection when the glass started to fly. I was sure the glass was going to shatter and that the shards would cut me in a hundred places.

Throughout the afternoon I had watched the clouds gathering and rolling toward my mountain. The (other) lookouts all chattered about it (on the radio). "Nestors'" (one of the Lookout group in my area I keep in touch with) caught the first wave of the storm, a tough cascade of gusts that passed in a few hours.

Next (the storm hit) "Dymond Gap" (lookout). She came down from her 108-foot watchtower to the ground cabin at dinner-time and sat the storm out there. No rain, she said, which was disappointing to the fire crews. It was getting toward the end of August and the forests were drying out. On the up side, there was no lightning either.

I signed off at 9pm as usual, just as the first gusts hit (Grayback Mt). Dry grasses and small bits of pumice showered the windows in brief spurts. The anemometer spun fast, then faster, then slower, then fast again. In the gathering dusk, the whirling blades glinted and I thought how handy it would be to have a windmill for electricity.

Even though it was August, the late day clouds had checked the heat and now the wind was making the little cabin downright chilly. I pulled on long pants, a long-sleeved shirt, and a sweater. A little hot tea would help. I decided to read a while and then cozy into my blankets, hoping the wind would lull me to sleep.

Just about the time I finished my first cup, the gusts kicked up. Now the splatter of debris against the windows was a constant clatter, simply louder or softer as the quantity of flung (flying) junk in the air fluctuated. I was glad that the two little windows that opened were on the north and south sides, rather than the west from where the wind was launching its assault. I could imagine the wind's invisible, insidious fingers jockeying the latch and hurling a window open, then chasing through the tiny cabin like a poltergeist, flinging papers, tin ware, pens, and books to the floor.

At first I was entertained by this uptick in the storm's intensity. What girl doesn't like a little flirt with danger in the dark? But after a while, it was less amusing than unnerving. It sounded like bucketsful of grit were colliding with my windows. I expected to discover, when morning came, that the panes had been sanded into frosted glass. Sometimes something with greater mass hit the windows, making me jump. I gathered the blanket around me and sat on the bunk.

The wind moaned and shrieked. The antennas on the roof whipped wildly, and sometimes colluded with the wind to whistle, an eerie, ghost-town sound. All the while debris battered the windows and hammered at the milk cans on the catwalk. One can was half-empty and sounded like a gong being rubbed rather than struck, a lingering, resonant undertone.

The gusts intensified again and now I thought I could see the panes shift a little within the narrow-slatted frames, flexing a bit as they resisted the violent shove from the wind. That's when I slid down onto the floor, pulling the blanket over my head. I got some more clothes out of the drawers and stuffed them inside the blanket, next to my shoulders and head, a little extra padding in case the glass really did give out.

By now I was convinced that it was just a matter of minutes before the windows yielded and glass and dirt and clumps of sagebrush would rain down on me. Despite being low to the ground and bolted to its cinderblock base, the lookout shimmied and shook. I curled into a ball, hoping that whatever struck my back wouldn't be too pointed or too long.

The floor was cold. The heater had gone out, the pilot snuffed by the relentless wind. I found my wool cap and put it on. Rocking a bit for warmth, I huddled and waited.

Sometimes the wind's voice softened to an almost sultry cadence in a brief lull, but then it escalated to banshee levels, screaming and tearing at the walls. I kept thinking, this is just a storm, it's just the wind, and it's just a few gusts. Thinking in terms of "justs" kept me from screaming out loud.

I kept rocking, kept whispering a mantra of "justs," sometimes counting off the seconds in each lull and taking advantage of these tiny respites to take a few deep breaths.

And so it went for several hours. I fell asleep in spite of the din and the battering. When I woke, all was quiet. The glass was intact in all the windows. I got the pilot relit on the heater and soon warmth was reaching into all corners of the cabin. I remade my bed and got in, still wearing all my clothes and the wool hat. For a while I lay still listening to the silence. There wasn't even a whisper of wind outside.

In the morning, the top of Grayback was scrubbed of most anything that had been loose. Small drifts of dirt had collected behind the stringers of the stairs. The outhouse door had been jiggled open and dust layered the seat and the toilet paper on its peg. Inside the weather station, all the instruments were coated with fine powder.

I swept, dusted, and shook out things under the blue sky. I let the rhythm of the broom un-jangle my nerves. The windows were not even scratched. I polished them clean with scrunched up newspapers and white vinegar.

By midday, the cabin was tidy again. As terrifying as the night had been, the new day was calm, even soothing. I made tea and sat in the sun, reveling in the clear air, fear forgotten again.

(Published with permission of the Author)

Forest Service Lookout:
Fact Verses Myth

Jumpoff Lookout

Mike Hiler

Few Forest Service symbols evoke more mystique than the lonely fire lookout station and the men and women who worked there. Though most of the old fire watch stations have vanished from the Northwest landscape, they remain a universal symbol of Forest Service history when pack strings, crank telephones, and crosscut saws were as common as computers and shiny SUV's are today.

Much of the mythology of the old lookouts is simply the way we choose to remember those times and not necessarily the way it really was. I worked on a lookout from 1969 to 1973 and what I remember is very different from the stories of lookouts spending long, leisurely days reading books in remote and often lonely stations.

In fact, my days at Jumpoff Lookout on the Naches Ranger District seemed quite the opposite. My log-book showed regular visits from hunters and hikers and the occasional concerns and ideas of the cowboys which I dutifully passed on to my supervisor. The stories and local lore that was passed on to me over a cup of coffee there remain my favorite memory

A typical day on the lookout included monitoring the radio 12 hours a day and logging calls. Sometimes this was a challenge. In the solitude of a lookout station, the outhouse should have been no problem but likely as not, if I tried to dash the 25 yards to the half-moon, I would be interrupted by an urgent radio call, an unexpected visitor, or my boss calling on the crank phone.

Each day I recorded and called in several weather readings, practiced fire finder skills, reported unusual cloud formations or changes in wind, and prepared three meals a day. Any spare moments were spent in learning the names and locations of local peaks and valleys, ridges and lakes. It was also necessary to keep the cramped living quarters neat and to keep all those windows clean so I could keep an eye on a half million acres where smoke could pop up at any time, day or night. Other duties included garbage patrol, packing out bags of litter for the general area, maintaining my single wire phone line and fire finder, and keeping track of the brands on the local cattle in case of trespass. Since I was supplied with only one milk can of water a week for washing, I carried water every day from a small spring. Of course springs are always downhill from lookout stations, making water hauling a chore.

Many August days turned into 24-hour marathons where an afternoon thunderclap would extend into a midnight lightning storm. I learned to balance a quick nap with other duties during those times. Sometimes my work actually included firefighting duties when lightning struck within hiking distance of the lookout. In those days (1969), the "lookout fire guard" was assigned a fire pack, including a crosscut saw, and was expected to keep the station axe sharp with the government regulation whetstone.

To be truthful, even though life on the lookout was certainly full, there was still time to simply enjoy the view. After all, I was there 24 hours a day, seven days a week, all summer. I do fondly remember the clear crisp air, unequaled sunrises and sunsets, the anticipation of an approaching storm, the wind picking up in the afternoon, huge cumulous clouds that seemed to boil in from outer space, and lazy raptors catching thermals in an effortless ballet of wings. In between storms there were long, slow afternoons when the buzzing of a few bottle flies against the window panes would announced that time was standing still.

However, in 1974 when a Wilderness ranger job opened up on the Tieton District in the Cougar Lakes backcountry, I jumped at the job. I figured hiking with a 55 pound pack over steep mountainous country for days at a time just sounded a whole lot easier...and it was.

* Cascade lookout magazine, 2005, USDA Forest Service

Ten Years on a Mountain Lookout,

Chapter One - Timberwolf Lookout

Unpublished diary, Forest Service archives

Mildred McMurray

We're told to "lift up our eyes to the mountains from whence cometh our help".

For that reason we came to the mountain top that first year, and since then, for six years we have returned each summer because we love it. The inspiration received from the scenery spread out below and above us, would be enough, but we have a never ending study of wildlife, wild flowers, birds, rocks and people.

We can drive to Timberwolf, or I should say we drive to it the last half of fire season. Before that, everyone walks from the snow bank—straight up for a quarter mile.

When we arrive to open the station, there are always huge snowbanks, sometimes 17 feet deep, extending from the bend of the road where one first comes into view of our station, the entire quarter mile to it and beyond.

It's always a gala day when the road is opened through, because that means plenty of water to use, and not a feeling of guilt from using wood and water that Harry must carry up on his back.

As we climb the trail to the little 14' x 14' building that serves us as our shelter for nearly three months during the summer, we feel that warm glow that comes when a traveler returns home from a long trip, "it's good to be home". We're back for another season.

Opening a station for the season is not fun. There are usually several of the boys from the ranger station to help with the job. Our things must all be carried up the hill via the backpack. The shutters must be opened and made fast, stove connected. Incidentally the first fire built after the winter's greasing nearly suffocates one; however, even that does some good because usually the building is filled with huge flies that have crawled in through cracks and they are glad to make a quick exit when the smoke rolls from the stove. The radio must be installed and tuned; the telephone must be working properly. That always takes about 2 days in advance, working the telephone line. Usually much of the line is lying on the ground, due to the winter snows. The anemometer must be installed atop a 25 foot pole and then connected so it will ring for wind speed. Next the weather station must be set up and a new sock put on the wet bulb. The dry sticks laid across the wire holder, for they must be right out in the weather where they will absorb any moisture that might come our way, or, get all the benefit of the sunshine and wind, to fully represent the duff on the forest floor.

Yes, it's a rush and a hustle by all who are doing the job, each having their own to do. Eventually it is done with the crew leaving the station, hiking down the hill, getting into their cars and driving on down the 13 miles to the Tieton Ranger Station.

We sink down on a chair to catch our breath and strength flows back in us as we view the inspiring panorama spread out before us.

Timberwolf Lookout station is situated on a mountain of the same name. It is so situated that it overlooks the Rattlesnake canyon, where the Rattlesnake River head high up in a canyon to the west of Rattlesnake Peaks, and we can follow its course all the way out to Washington State Route 410, excepting for a short distance where it encircles our mountain to the northwest. As it travels, it grows with various other streams emptying into it until by the time the North Fork joins it, the Rattlesnake has become a good sized river. Reports have it that fishing is fine, especially in the upper reaches of the river. I suppose the reason for that is due to the fact that only a few hardy individuals ever take the 4 ½ mile trip, hiking with a pack via the MJB trail each year. Some day we hope to try it with horses.

Paralleling the upper Rattlesnake River to the north of it we turn to another rugged canyon, the Hindoo. It is even a more primitive area than the upper Rattlesnake. One branch, the Big Hindoo heads back of Mt. Aix and Bismarck Peak. The other one, the Little Hindoo, heads north of the Rattlesnake Peaks, joining as they rush down the canyon to pour into the Rattlesnake River. We have good reports on the fishing in there too, of course, for the same reason the upper Rattlesnake is good.

Our eyes follow up the tree covered ridges and come to rest on a sight that thrills and stirs the soul of the most calloused individual who came to visit the lookout station. The upper half of Mt. Rainier looms up to our west over nearby Nelson Ridge with lessor peaks up to 7800 feet altitude, reminding one of a foreboding old mother hen hovering over and protecting her young. Her dignity is outstanding among glacier covered mountains, and beauty unexcelled. To me, a veil of mystery surrounds this mountain, perhaps because it is involved in so many of the old Indian legends.

To our southwest, Mt. Adams stands very stately and beautiful, covered with a white mantel.

Just right of Mt. Adams is Goat Rocks. It is a hauntingly beautiful and rugged wilderness area that became familiar to many through Justice William O. Douglas's book, *Of Men and Mountains.*

As I sit here gazing out across the 22 air miles that separate them from Timberwolf, Gilbert Peak raises its head above the rest. Harry and I reflect on the man from who it derives its name, Curtis Gilbert, a great Boy Scout leader and citizen. He loved the Goat Rocks and had used Gilbert Peak as a goal to climb with scouts a number of times. Very fittingly his ashes rest over the mountain he loved so well.

I can see just a bit farther when I look at the Goat Rocks. In my mind's eye I see a mountain meadow, green as emeralds, filled with brooks and wildflowers. It is surrounded by high mountain walls over which water cascades into a falls. We fed our horses there and named it Shangri La Meadows.

We get just a teasing glimpse of Mt. St. Helens. Our McNeil Peak in the foreground hides it, but we can still say that we see it.

To our north, we see the very rugged and picturesque range of mountains by Salmon La Sac. And still beyond them, 96 air miles from Timberwolf stands pure white Glacier Peak. She is located in the southern part of Mt. Baker National Forest.

On to the east of north, we have the rugged range of mountains in the Wenatchee National Forest, with Mt. Stewart standing far above them all. These are our high peaks. These are beautiful inspirational mountains that give a spiritual uplift to all who gaze on their height.

We suddenly come to our senses and realize we have a real job awaiting us in finding a place for belongings in this 14' x 14' room where we live around the fire finder.

Timberwolf is one lookout that can boast of a cellar. We don't know how we could get along without it. This was dug out and built by the 1st lookout here, a one-armed man. It is used as a clothes closet, storage space, and cooler. Above all, it is now packrat free. Our first year here it was not, and one of the too friendly fellows proceeded to make fringe all around Harry's red wool jacket by taking little bites from the bottom. That's all he could reach.

By bedtime we are quite exhausts from our opening day on Timberwolf and are quite ready to retire; but wait, how can one get undressed before those bare, dark windows that are continuous all around the building, with no shades? That feeling soon left when the shades of night lowered. It is amazing how soundly one can sleep on the mountain top. In the quiet tranquility of it all, one can but realize, "God is in his Heaven, all's right with the world".

Dawn comes up like thunder. The sun shines in the window on you as it appears above the horizon and you are privileged to greet it (the most beautiful time of the day) in quiet solitude. It seems almost a sacrilege to speak aloud or to make any unnecessary noises. More often than not, we see wildlife of some sort near the station when we go out for our first early morning check. The mountain peaks, tops of the trees, even rocks become magic by the sun's first rays.

Thus day has come to Timberwolf and with the day the beginning of our year's duty as a team of Fire Guards in the Snoqualmie National Forest. We take our job seriously, because we feel we are performing an important part in keeping Washington green.

Not only do we feel we are helping to preserve our forests for our grandchildren, but we hope for their grandchildren too, because we have learned to love the forests, mountains and streams all that live therein. This is why as visitors come here in search of beauty as an antidote for the pressures of present day living, we try to convey to them the importance of our watersheds. Every single person must do his part in helping conserve them. We point out to them the problems of the countries and part of our own United States that have not. We try to make it clear that supervised logging is as a farmer choosing that produce which is ripe and ready for harvest. How the logging roads are used by fire suppression crews, thus making a speedier trip to a fire. Also, they act as a fire break, and give John Q. Public the privilege of traveling safely high in the mountains. People are appreciating more and more of our great heritage and express themselves freely on the subject.

Harry usually goes to the spring for water immediately after the first check look of the day. Nearly the entire first half of our season we must walk the last quarter mile to the station, which is due to the fact our roadway is one solid mass of snowbank, some parts of which are 17 feet high. Of course, during that time, getting water is not the pleasure it becomes later on, for every drop of water must be carried up the steep incline past the snowbank, on our backs, as well as our firewood and all else we brought up to the station.

The spring itself is 1 ½ miles from our lookout and lies in a pleasant little meadow-like spot. Harry has enclosed the spring itself with a husky log fence and has covered and piped the water to a distance of about fifteen feet from the enclosure where it gushes out into a deep ditch lined with flat rocks and he fills his water cans with the delicious, clear, very cold water of the mountains.

I think breakfast is the most enjoyable meal of the day on our mountain top. Probably because it comes in the cool of the morning and the (clear air over the) mountain peaks are their clearest. Of course, the exercise of climbing hills with a heavy pack could be a factor too; but I do know there is nothing to compare with the aroma of coffee in the making and bacon frying. That alone can whet one's appetite to the maximum. After breakfast is over, and our daily devotional read, our duties of the day are faced with a new zest.

We have hourly check-looks to make, but after spending some time on a lookout, our eyes maintain an almost constant vigil for anything that is different on our landscape and might spell smoke. In other words we train our eyes to REALLY SEE.

One of the first duties of a lookout each year is to tune of his fire finder, even as a civil engineer levels and orients his instrument to known points. Another early job for a new lookout is to study his map and learn his surrounding territory such as all the ravines, ridges, roads, streams, mountain peaks or any other descriptive landmark. The better he knows his country, the more efficient job he can do. But, as fire detection needs a chapter of its own, I will go into that later.

A genuine house cleaning comes with the opening of the station; that means the many windows to was, inside and outside. Of course this job must be repeated often through the season, for our job is to see, therefore clean windows are important.

A recording of the weather must be taken three times a day and sent into two stations. The relative humidity is determined by reading a dry and wet bulb (thermometers) and referring to a chart. The dry sticks are weighed on a scale for the purpose. They are 4 dowel-like kiln dried ponderosa pine sticks, fastened together parallel, and laid across two wire holders six inches from the ground, out in the weather at all times to fully represent the percent of fuel moisture on the forest floor. We must determine the state of weather, amount of clouds, visibility and read the anemometer for wind speed, also the directional indicator for the direction from which the wind is blowing.

From the percentage of fuel moisture and the speed of the wind we learn the class of day. We keep these records in our own weather book for the season to turn into our office when we are through up here. Also, we keep a daily log of all conversation on the radio and phone pertaining to business and it MUST be only business on the radio, but for a 15 minute "gab session" at night for each district.

We must check the one man fire pack to see that it is in proper working order and all items are there.

We establish a "deep freeze" in our closest deep snowbank and can keep frozen packages of meat frozen hard for a week and milk sweet for a good two weeks, so the snowbanks are pretty important to we who have to stay up here several weeks at a time.

We must learn each year anew, how to cook and bake in our little wood stove, and usually burn a couple batches of biscuits before re-learning the technique.

175

Our little lawn must be watered each day because on the very top of the mountain it is dry. Harry hauls snow via the wheelbarrow each evening and piles it over the entire yard; by morning there is usually some snow left, but it is nice and damp. The grass usually suffers a bit before all the snow goes off the road so we can drive up because it is too long and steep a haul for the wheelbarrow with Harry pushing, as the pickup cannot as yet be driven through.

With no warning, visitors may arrive, their numbers according to the weather. Our time is theirs (unless we have a fire or a storm at the time) to answer all questions and show them about the country from Timberwolf, to help them enjoy more fully, to the full extent of our knowledge, their trip up here. Fore surely they love the wilderness, or they wouldn't undertake the long dusty trip over steep mountain roads.

Thus a typical day without storms or smokes has ended. The sun slips down behind Mt. Rainier, often with a beautiful sunset, lingering as though it hated to leave.

Then the air comes alive with the "gab session" with everyone trying to get acquainted with others they will be working with all season. Knowing, but probably never meeting face-to-face, for many boys from the east are stationed on lookouts and they leave early in the season. We have met some very outstanding people, via the Federal radio system.

Unpublished memories, U. S. Forest Archives

Appendix A

Lookouts by Access Type
Naches Ranger District

The lookouts in this guide are reached by roads leading to trails in the Naches Basin. All sites are approached west of Naches (WA) from Highway 12 and Highway 410, east on highway 410 from Enumclaw, or east on Highway 12 from Packwood. Most trips generally take a full day of exploring while some trips can be extended with alternate suggested routes, camping, or by walking slower.

FOREST ROAD ACCESS

- Big Bald Mountain Lookout FROM Highway 410 AT Sprick Park, gravel road requires strong tires

- Raven Roost Lookout: FROM Highway 410 and onto Little Naches Forest Road #1902 for13 miles

- Timberwolf Lookout FROM either Highway 410 or 12 by way of forest Road #1500 to the lookout spur

FOUR-WHEEL DRIVE ACCESS, most difficult

- Blue Slide Lookout FROM Ahtanum North Fork past Tampico, by way of Darland Mountain Lookout

- Cleman Mountain Lookout, FROM Hwy 410 by way of Bald Mountain Road

- Darland Mountain Lookout FROM Tampico over diverse 4x4 jeep type road system

- Clover Springs Lookout FROM Nile area or Cliffdell over Clover Springs Road and 4x4 jeep type segments

- Jumpoff Lookout Station FROM Windy Point on Highway 12 over thirteen mile 4x4 route

- Little Bald Lookout FROM Cliffdell on challenging forest roads

- Miners Ridge Lookout FROM Bumping Lake by way of Bumping Lake Road #1808

- Quartz Mountain Lookout FROM Cle Elum through Taneum Basin or Ellensburg through Manastash Basin

MOTORIZED BIKE TRAIL ACCESS

- Blue Slide Lookout FROM Rimrock Lake on climbing Short and Dirty Trail

- Quartz Mountain FROM Cle Elum by way of Taneum Road System or trails from Bald Mountain Lookout

TRAILS ACCESS, NON WILDERNESS

- Cleman Mountain Lookout: Steep Waterworks Trail from near junction of Highways 12 and 410

- Devils Slide, FROM Highway 410 on Gold Creek Road and Trail or from Bald Mountain Lookout Site

- Edgar Rock Lookout FROM Lost Creek Village Trailhead or Forest Road #1706

- Jumpoff Lookout FROM Long Lake Trailhead via Louie Gap or 13 mile Jumpoff dirt road.

- Pyramid Peak Lookout FROM Pyramid Pass accessed from Greenwater or Little Naches Road systems

WILDERNESS ACCESS: FOOT TRAILS

- American Ridge Lookout (Goat Peak) FROM Highway 410 or Bumping Lake Road on steep system trails

- Arch Rock Shelter Site FROM Government Meadows or Pyramid Pass over the PCT

- Bear Creek Mountain Lookout FROM Pinegrass Ridge by way of Rimrock Lake.

- Crystal Peak Lookout FROM Crystal Mountain Road off Highway 410 or by PCT from Chinook Pass

- Mt. Aix Lookout FROM trailheads near Bumping Lake or McDaniel Lake over both ends of the same trail

- Round Mountain Lookout FROM Clear Lake Spur Road or from the PCT south of White Pass

- Tumac Mountain Lookout FROM trailheads near White Pass or Deep Creek in Bumping Lake Basin.

PRITE LAND OWNERSHIP, Enter with Permission only

- Bald Mountain Lookout FROM Sprick Park or connecting roads and trails off Highway 410

- Pine Mountain Lookout: State DNR Managed private land, requires authorization from land owner

GPS BUSHWHACKING OPPORTUNITIES

- Jumpoff Lookout FROM road ends near Lost Lake to connecting game trails

- American Ridge Lookout (Goat Peak) from Chipmunk Road #1802 off Bumping River Road #`800

APPENDIX B

MOUNTAIN PEAK ESTIMATED ELEVATIONS AND POTENTIAL VIEW POINTS TO VISIT NACHES RANGER DISTRICT

Name	Elevation	Location
Arch Rock	5080 estimated	T18N, R11E, sec 22 (proposed site)
Arnesons Peak	6450	T14N, R12E, Sec. 11
Bald Mt # 9	5900 estimated	T17N, R15E, Sec. 15 (Lookout Site)
Bear Creek Mt # 15	7336 estimated	T12N, R12E, Sec. 17 (Lookout Site)
Bethel Ridge	6223	Up there Somewhere
Bismark Peak	7585	T15N, R12E, Sec. 30
Blowout	5320 estimated	T19N, R11E, Sec. 14
Blue Slide # 1	6785	T12N, R12E, Sec. 4 (Lookout Site)
Burnt Mountain	6536	T14N, R13E, Sec. 15
Chimney Peaks	3870	T13N, R14E, Sec. 3

Name	Elevation	Location
Cleman Lookout # 10	5115 estimate	T15N, R16E, Sec 5 (lookout Site)
Clover Springs # 18	6351	T16N, R13E, Sec. 22 (Lookout Site)
Crag Mountain	6208	T15N, R11E, Sec. 22
Cramer Mountain	5992	T14N, R11E, Sec. 23
Crown Point	5870	T17N, R11E, Sec. 31
Darland # 11	697 ?	T11N, R13E, Sec. 20 (Lookout Site)
Devil's Horns	7090	T12N, R11E, Sec. 19
Devils Slide	3526	T17N, R15E, Sec. 17
Dog	7041	T15N, R13E, Sec. 9
Dome Peak	6591	T13N, R14E, Sec. 32
Edgar Rock # 3	3620 estimated.	T17N, R14E, Sec. 26 (Lookout Site)
Fifes Peaks	6954	T17N, R12E, Sec. 11
Gilbert Peak	8201	T12N, R11E, Sec. 35
Goat Peak # 17	6473 estimated	T17N, R13E, Sec. 19 (Lookout Site)
Goose Egg	4500	T14N, R14E, Sec. 32
Hogback	6789	T13E, R11E, Sec. 22
Ironstone	6441	T14N, R13E, Sec. 19

Name	Elevation	Location
Ives Peak	7380	T12N, R11E, Sec. 28
Jumpoff Lookout # 4	5745	T13N, R14E, Sec. 1 (Station)
Kloochman Rock	4532	T13N, R14E, Sec. 9
Little Bald # 5 (Lookout Site)	6104 estimated	T16N, R13E, Sec. 2
McNeil Peak	6658	T14N, R12E, Sec. 13
Meeks Table	4500	T15N, R13E, Sec. 18
Name	Elevation	Location
Miners Ridge # 6 (Lookout Site)	6072 erstimated	T15N, R11E, Sec. 12
Mount Aix # 19 (Lookout Site)	7779 estimated	T15N, R13E, Sec. 18
Mount Clifty	6245	T19N, R13E, Sec. 25
Naches Peak	6457	T16N, R10E, Sec. 18
Nelson Butte	7200	T15N, R13E, Sec. 3
Norse Peak # 21 (Lookout Site)	6858 estimated	T17N, R11E, Sec. 17
Old Scab	6642	T16N, R13E, Sec. 9
Old Snowy	7930	T12N, R11E, Sec. 21
Panther Ridge	5699	T19N, R14E, Sec. 31
Pear Butte	6438	T15N, R12E, Sec. 34

Name	Elevation	Location
Pyramid Peak # 13	5715 estimated	T19N, R11E, Sec. 28 (Lookout Site)
Quartz Mountain # 14	6290 estimated	T18N, R14E, Sec. 3 (Lookout Site)
Rattlesnake Peaks	6850	T14N, R13E, Sec. 32
Raven Roost # 7	6199, present site 6179 ?	T18N, R12E, Sec. 22 (Lookout Site)
Red Rock	4478	T15N, R14E, Sec. 21
Round Mt. # 16	5976 ??	T13N, R12E, Sec. 9 (Lookout Site)
Shellrock Peak # 24	5920	T14N, R12E, Sec. 32
Tieton Peak	7768	T12N, R11E, Sec. 24
Timberwolf Mountain #8	6391 ? estimated	T15N, R13E, Sec. 25 (Lookout Site)
Tumac Mountain #20	6340 est: Lewis Co.	T14N, 12E, Sec 8 (Lookout site)
Yakima Peak	6231	T16N, R10E, Sec. 14

* All lookout elevations are taken from other sources or estimated as an average when those sources generally agree. Don't forget that the elevation of the geological peak and the floor of the lookouts are often different, sometimes by many feet. "No big deal" you say, but the Osborne Firefinder bases its' accuracy on the height of the actual placement and a few feet off might change a reading. If sources generally disagree I indicate with one question mark. I

designate "estimate" when there are differences in stated elevation. I've seen a number of stated elevations for Jumpoff Lookout, who knows which is the best? Perhaps someone will write a book about this issue some day but it won't be me.

Original list supplied by the Naches Ranger Station.

Thank you nameless former federal employee

for developing this original list on your time off

Appendix C

Getting Back

- Safe traveling on the National Forest Roads and Trails -

AND getting back home

Check List

The 10 essential lists

The " Basic" 10 Essentials for hiking, sometimes called the "And-Or" list

works best if you make up a "Big 10" bag

so you can keep it up to date and grab it on the run.

1. Hat or Cap (If your feet get cold, put on a cap, if your head gets cold, put on gloves)

2. Jacket or windbreaker and/or some rain protection (if your fingers are cold stuff in pockets)

3. Map and Compass

4. Water and extra food

5. Sun glasses and sun screen

6. * Sharp pocket knife and bottle opener (OR, a Swiss Army Knife)

7. Flashlight or headlamp and batteries

8. Matches and fire starter (toilet paper works well here, IF it's dry, Candle backs up TP)

9. Neckerchief or headband or scarf

10. First Aid Kit and tweezers and/or some first aid supplies

(Don't forget to have a list of Ten Essentials in the ten essentials bag for a reminder and updating)

The Extra essentials (making up the 20 essentials)

11. Cell phone (with CHARGED battery). Times change, get used to it.

12. Rope, chord, tyvek sheet or ground cloth, plastic, or poncho

13. Gloves (if your head is cold put on gloves)

14. Magnifying glass

15. Tape Measurer (35 feet to document large trees)

16. * A strong sheath knife

17. A strong walking stick

18. Signal mirror even if you don't know how to use it, you'll figure it out if needed

19. TP, in a zip lock bag to keep it dry (good fire starter)

20. Garden trowel to bury human waste

AND, in case you forgot - The 24 Essentials

- Swiss Army type scissors

- Needle and Thread

- GPS and batteries with GPS instructions

- A note book and pencil (to jot down GREAT poems or take notes on big trees)

Pack String Essentials

1. Shovel (trowel)

2. Bucket

3. Ax or hatchet (sharpened), or camp saw

4. Large flashlight

5. Coffee, sugar cubes, and can of condensed milk (or extra food)

6. Jug (once called a canteen) of water and drinking cup

Essentials for Visiting Lookouts and Viewpoints

- A good windbreaker

- Binoculars

- A good cap with earflaps and visor

- Sun Glasses

- Notebook and small measuring tape (for repair notes)

- Camera to document items of work

- Most hikers who visit lookouts wear clothing

The Forest Road Trip Essentials:

- 12 volt auto air compressor, condensed in size (yes, I've actually used this)

- Jumper Cables and/or jumper battery device. Store in spare tire rim

- Blanket

- Money

- Water jug and cup

- Roll of TP (Don't count on any forest toilet to supply anything beyond a hole)

   TP can double as a fire starter or sanitary first-aid wipe

- Tire chains optional, all times of the year or drive judicially

-   **Before you leave home**

-   - Does someone know where you are?

-   - Check your spare tire air pressure

-   - Is your water fresh

-   - Is your drinking water bottle leaking, is the cap tight?

-   - Have mice chewed on your candy bar, tent, or pack? (or, is a mouse living in your pack)?

-   - Is your map current

To make your trip more enjoyable:

1. Something to read, Kindle light's work great if they are charged

2. Camera (often known to annoy others in your party, be judicious about holding up your group

   someone has probably already photographed THAT flower!)

3. Both a brim hat and an "ear warm" cap

4. No other device make you as safe as a hiking partner

AND

- The Boy Scout Motto is always a good standby: **Be Prepared**

- Might as well have all your battery devices use the same size batteries, preferably AA

- * You can purchase a small, diamond edge knife sharpener. Whetstones are heavy!

- One challenge is remembering that the weather at your home and the weather on the Cascade Crest

> (or atop most mountains and lookouts) can be radically different. Also, weather is generally

> more severe at higher elevations, and winds seem to hover along peaks and ridges.

> Wind can be hazardous on clear sunny days, cloudy days, and in rain or snow storms.

- Larger flashlights always work better than small ones, but in most cases, a small flashlight

> is all you need, EXCEPT when you are trying to attract attention or pack a horse

> or change a tire. Sometimes, when returning late, 30 minutes of flashlight will substitute

> for sleeping in a log.

- What is your plan if your reading glasses are lost or broken?

- If you are lost, you are more likely confused in your mind. Carry a deck of cards:

> If you get lost start playing solitaire and someone will eventually look over your shoulder

> and say "Did you think of putting that card over there?" Then, ask the butinski the way home.

After it's all said and done I have found the most "helpful mantra" to repeat when lost is:

When you're lost
Or in doubt,
Run in circles,
Scream and Shout.

* See Also::   - Hiler, Mike, *Choosing a Knife for Backpacking* , Signpost Magazine April, 199

Appendix D

Wilderness Ethics and Woodsy Owl leave no trace Practices

Leave No Trace

Pack it in, Pack it out.

Bury human waste several inches in an inconspicuous location AND mark with a stick cross to avoid conflicts with other hikers, or just pack it home

If you packed it in, you can more easily pack it out

It's easier to carry an empty can than a full can.

Your mother won't be visiting the Wilderness this year, You'll have to pack out your own trash!

Leave the boom box home. If music you must, use ear buds. Yes, it's annoying.

Take only photos, leave only footprints

(AND, again)
The Boy Scout Motto
"Be Prepared"

Appendix E

Lookout Anomalies

Peak Elevations:

Mountain peak elevations hardly ever agree among the various sources available. Some of that may be attributed to older measurements which were updated, confused, mistaken, and who knows what. Also, to make the Osborne Fire Finder work more accurately, the Individual lookouts generally attempted to use the height of the lookout floor in calculations rather than the height of the host peak. I have attempted to place a general average when common references generally agree. See Appendix B for my best estimate and an additional note on discrepancies.

Lookouts occasionally have an alternative name, Including:

- "Jumpoff lookout is the official name but is often called "Jumpoff Joe". There are at least

   two actual "Jumpoff Joe" Lookouts, one in Columbia Valley and one in Oregon.

- Pine Mountain is sometimes called Cowiche Lookout or Cowiche Mountain Lookout

- Clover Springs was occasionally called Soda Spring Lookout

- Crystal Peak Lookout, Crystal Lake Lookout, and Crystal Point Lookouts are all the same place

- Little Bald Mountain was originally "Bald Mountain", and later, "Old Baldy by Jack Nelson

There are a number of different lookouts which share a common name.

Name	Shared With
- Goat Peak -	(American Ridge):

- Goat Peak in Okanogan and another in Kittitas Counties,

- Goat Butte in Yakima Co.

- Goat Mountain in Okanogan, Whitcom, and King Counties.

- Miners Ridge:	- Miners Ridge in Snohomish County
- Quartz Mountain:	- Spokane and Ferry Counties
- Pyramid Peak:	- Pyramid Mountain near Lake Crescent in Chelan County
- Big and Little Bald Mountain:	-Baldy in Chelan, and Pend Oreille Counties
	- Little Baldy Peak in Skamania County
	- Old Baldy in Okanogan County
	-South Baldy in Pend Orielle
-Jumpoff Ridge	- Ridge north of Wenatchee , WA, no connection to Jumpoff Lookout

BIBLIOGRAPHY

- Abbott, A. T., *Tumac Mountain: A Post Glacial Cinder Cone in Washington State*, U. of W. 1951

- Abbott, A. T., *The Geology of the Northwest Portion of Mt. Aix Quadrangle*,

- Washington, U. of W. PH. D. Thesis, 1953. See: pp. 136-47

- Carter, Susan, *Forest Service Administrative History, Wenatchee National Forest*, DRAFT, Wenatchee, WA. 1992

- Cyr, Suzy, *Tanum, the Story of Bumping Lake*, on Amazon, 2022

- *- Douglas, William O, *Of Men and Mountains,* 1951 Harper and Brothers, NY.

- Goeff, Clayton, *Geology of White Pass, Tumac Mt. Area*, Washington U. of W. 1980 (State DNR, Earth Sciences)

- * Gossett, Gretta Petersen, *Beyond the Bend*, Ye Galleon Press, 1979.

- Hiler, Mike, *Mt. Aix*, Signpost Magazine, March, 1989.

- Hiler, Mike, *Buckskin Larch and Bedrock*, Cave Moon Press, 2011

- Holland, Andy, *Switchbacks*, Mountaineers, Seattle, WA. 1980.

- * Kresek, Ray, *Fire Lookouts of the Northwest*, Ye Galleon Press, Fairfield, Washington, 1984.

- * Miles, Jo, *Kamiakin Country*, Caxton Press, Caldwell, ID, 2017

- * Nelson, Jack, *We Never Got Away*, Franklin Press 1965, Yakima

- Simpson, Charles D. & Jackman, E.R., *Blazing Forest Trails*, The Caxton Printers, Ltd., Caldwell, ID. 1967.

- - * Splawn, A.J. *Kamiakin*, Caxton Press, 1917

- - * Spring, Ira & Fish, Byron, *Lookouts: Firewatchers of the Cascades and Olympics*, The Mountaineers, Seattle, WA 1981

* Good reading on local history and lore

VIDEOS

- The Construction of Round Mountain Lookout, 1948, Arneson. Naches Ranger District Video Library.

INTERVIEWS AND PERSONAL COLLECTIONS

- Howatt, Packy. Interview, Hiler, Naches Ranger Station, 1988.

WEB SITES

- National Lookout Assn. web site: Good for finding information on a specific lookout quickly or for joining this fine organization.

- "Washington lookouts.weebly.com": Good for finding a lookout quickly, interactive so help these guys with your trips.

- Former fire lookout sites register:

- Good for GPS coordinates, works from a map so might help to nearby sites?

- National Lookout Assn. web site, good for finding a lookout quickly, joining the National Association,   or   current   lookout news.

BONUS POEM

And thus,

I finish my description of the lookouts,

former lookouts, almost lookouts, and not quite lookouts

as well as other stories

of the Naches Basin and surrounding ridges,

spilling over to other areas and other times

with each their own story

(yet to be told)

(and as the stories slowly fade into myth).

/mh

Meet the Author

Mike Hiler is a ceramic artist who lives in Washington State with his wife, Kristin Hiler. He is a former public school teacher, fire lookout, Wilderness Ranger and managed National Forest Wilderness in the Washington Cascades for a number of years. Mike and his son, Matt, nominated a former National Register champion Big Mt. Hemlock, located near Mt. Aix, WA. Mike is active in raising Milk Weed seed to improve and support Migrating Monarch Butterfly populations though the Cowiche Canyon Conservancy in Yakima, Washington. Mike and Kristin are fire lookout volunteers at Red Top Lookout near Cle Elum, WA when the station is in operation. They also help maintain Jumpoff Lookout, near Yakima, WA for for ongoing open public access.

Also by Mike Hiler

Poetry Collections
- Sticks: 1977

- Logbook: Small press release, 1988

- Journey: TapJoe Journal release, (Backpack edition), 1992

- Buckskin Larch and Bedrock: Cave moon Press, 2011

- Listos: Cave Moon Press, 2017

Lookouts and History

- "Study Guide for the Naches Pass Trail", Yakima Valley Museum, 1989

- Mike has contributed a number of articles to the National Forest Fire Lookout Association Quarterly. Search

"Forest fire lookout" or: <u>www.fire</u>lookout.org" for more information about that important Association

- Mike contributed many Washington Trail and Wilderness History articles to the WTA magazine "Signpost", now out of print

Meet the story tellers

Wendy Warren: Wendy Warren is an artist and writer who lives in Yakima, Washington and served at Pine Mt Lookout and Gray Back Lookout (Klickitat County: T.6N R.14E S.20). Wendy is presently working on a book about her Lookout experiences.

Mildren McMurray: Mildred and her husband Harry worked on Timberwolf lookout for 10 years between 1951 and 1964. She wrote a very interesting story about those summers and chapter 1 of that unpublished book graces the following pages of this book. The rest of her unpublished book is housed at the Naches Ranger Station.

Publications by Cave Moon Press

FOR UNIVERSITIES AND MUSEUMS

FOR MIDDLE SCHOOL CHILDREN

POETS

www.ingramcontent.com/pod-product-compliance
Lightning Source LLC
Chambersburg PA
CBHW070803280326
41934CB00012B/3041